GLORY DAYS

Hants & Dorset

Ian Allan
PUBLISHING

James Prince

CONTENTS

First published 2006

ISBN (10) 0 7110 3105 3
ISBN (13) 978 0 7110 3105 0

All rights reserved. No part of this book
may be reproduced or transmitted in any
form or by any means; electronic or
mechanical, including photocopying,
recording or by any information storage
and retrieval system, without permission
from the Publisher in writing.

© Ian Allan Publishing Ltd 2006

Published by Ian Allan Publishing

an imprint of Ian Allan Publishing Ltd,
Hersham, Surrey KT12 4RG

Printed in England by Ian Allan Printing
Ltd, Hersham, Surrey KT12 4RG

Code: 0605/B1

Visit the Ian Allan Publishing website at
www.ianallanpublishing.com

The standard double-decker
of the 1930s was the Leyland
Titan. A typical example with
Leyland bodywork is seen here
splashing through part of
Southampton. *British
Commercial Vehicle Museum*

FOREWORD

A surprising number of the best-known bus and coach operators were founded in Bournemouth. Royal Blue, Shamrock & Rambler, Excelsior European Motorways, Charlie's Cars and, of course, Bournemouth Corporation spring to mind — as does Hants & Dorset Motor Services.

Having been born in Lyndhurst and brought up in Bournemouth, I have known Hants & Dorset ever since I can remember. However, it was the Corporation's yellow Leylands and Daimlers that started my interest in buses, the H&D Bristols always seeming a bit special. The yellow buses were ridden on daily, the green only for those special trips to far-flung Poole or Wimborne.

As a youngster growing up in the 1970s I remember two things about Hants & Dorset (or 'pants & corset', as my father insisted on calling it), these being the change from Tilling green to National Bus Company poppy red and the disastrous bus-station fire, two events that changed the face of the organisation.

For many the 'glory days' ended around this time, but it is easily forgotten that more than 35 years have passed since the National Bus Company (NBC) was formed, and many enthusiasts have grown up knowing little else. Also, the sheer variety of vehicles acquired, both new and second-hand, make this one of the most interesting periods in the company's history, if not necessarily the most glorious. It is with this in mind that I have decided to end the book with the company split of 1983, when the Hants & Dorset name disappeared.

I only hope that you enjoy reading this book as much as I have enjoyed compiling it. The final version was possible only with the help of the many photographers who allowed me to use their pictures, to whom I extend my thanks, and of my good friend Keith Mitchell, whose assistance with historical data and knowing the answer to many of my questions was invaluable. To everyone who has contributed, thank you.

James Prince
Lytchett Matravers, Dorset
January 2006

3

1. BOURNEMOUTH & DISTRICT

By 1916 William Wells Graham had for more than 10 years been proprietor of the West Cliff garage in St Michael's Road, Bournemouth, and during this time he had built up a neat little sideline in car hire. One of his best customers was Walter Flexman French, a small but distinguished-looking silver-haired gentleman who often visited Bournemouth. A councillor for the London Borough of Wandsworth, French had been involved in bicycle manufacture, a business which had suffered since the repeal of the Red Flag Act in 1896. By 1899 he was operating a pair of Daimler Wagonettes on bus services in London, initially between Putney and Piccadilly and later from Streatham to Balham.

Something of an omnibus pioneer, French had retired from the cycle business in 1903 and become manager and engineer of the Sussex Motor Road Car Co. He quickly set about replacing the operator's steam buses with a fleet of new Milnes Daimlers and soon afterwards acquired the Worthing Motor Omnibus Co. The business expanded along the coast towards Portsmouth and Southampton, and in 1915 Worthing Motors, the London & South Coast Haulage Co and the country services of the Brighton, Hove & Preston United Omnibus Co were merged to form Southdown Motor Services.

Meanwhile, in 1908, a new company had started running a hired Darracq-Serpollet steam bus between Maidstone and Chatham. The venture was not a success, suffering severe financial problems, but French saw potential and purchased the business in 1910. He soon renamed it the Maidstone, Chatham, Gravesend & District Motor Omnibus Service and handed over day-to-day control to his son, George. The company was registered as The Maidstone & District Motor Services Ltd in March 1911. Matters improved to the extent that the British Electric Traction Company (BET) acquired an interest in M&D in 1913. This was not French's only dealing with BET, for in 1914 another of his companies, Guildford & District, was purchased by BET-owned Aldershot & District following a short period of competition.

Thus when Messrs French and Graham had a chat about the potential of longer-distance omnibus services around Bournemouth, Graham knew that French had some idea of what he was talking

about and that his already well-established business could form the nucleus of a new company.

Friends at BET were contacted. BET had already formed a new subsidiary, British Automobile Traction (BAT), to sponsor its bus interests, and plans were formulated to start a series of services which, when combined with other operators' routes, would form a network linking the South Coast with London.

Bournemouth & District Motor Services Ltd was registered as a private company on Friday 17 March 1916, with Walter Flexman French as Chairman. William Wells Graham, who continued to run his garage and car-hire business alongside the fledgling operation, was appointed Co-Director and General Manager, and the interests of BAT were represented by Sidney Garcke. Garcke soon retired from the company, and BAT's involvement was handled thereafter by his former colleague, James Spagnoletti. A Mr James MacKeekin of Ufford underwrote the company, which had a nominal capital of £30,000 (the equivalent of around £1,300,000 at 2006 values).

The first difficulty encountered — and one which is rather important in the provision of bus services — was the securing of suitable vehicles. Because of the 1914-18 war most chassis were earmarked for military service, but eventually four Straker-Squire chassis were acquired and fitted with charabanc bodies by Knight of Poole. They were finished in an aluminium livery and operated as the 'Silver Fleet'. Fleet numbers were used, but, to give the impression that the fleet was larger than it was, only even numbers were issued — a practice that was to continue until 1939.

Although it was good to have a smart fleet of new silver charabancs, the company had considerable difficulty obtaining stage-carriage licences. The initial plan was for a service to Lymington, a market town approximately 20 miles to the east of Bournemouth, followed by additional routes to Ringwood, Wimborne and Southampton. Negotiations had started the previous summer with Lymington Borough and Bournemouth Corporation, and, while Lymington recognised the advantages such a service would bring, Bournemouth Corporation was less keen, fearing increased competition for its own tram system.

Sea Corner, Highcliffe, in the early-1920s. Although still recognisable today, this road now forms the A337 trunk road between Christchurch and Lymington, whence the Leyland single-decker, with luggage being loaded on to the roof, had departed around an hour before the photograph was taken. *Classic Pictures*

While negotiations continued the Straker-Squires were employed on tours departing from Bournemouth Square, but more difficulties were encountered. Petrol rationing became stricter, and in 1917 two of the charabancs were requisitioned by the War Department, leaving the company with just two vehicles, which were themselves requisitioned later. In desperation the company pressed into service a pair of two-horse charabancs, and for a while these were its only vehicles. At least petrol rationing was no longer an issue! The Straker-Squires never returned to Bournemouth.

By 1918 the company still did not have a stage-carriage route, but in that year two small concerns that had been struggling to maintain services during the war years were ready to sell out. The Canford Cliffs Motor Omnibus Co and Eugene Poulain were both operating between County Gates and Sandbanks, inside the Poole boundary. In July Poulain's licences and vehicles were acquired, followed on 20 August by those of Canford Cliffs Motors. At last Bournemouth & District Motor Services had its first stage-carriage service, albeit across the county boundary, in Dorset.

A pair of De Dion Bouton 28-seat charabancs was acquired from Poulain and two Milnes Daimler buses from Canford Cliffs Motors. Early motor buses were notoriously troublesome, breakdowns occurring on an almost hourly basis, so replacements were quickly sought. Four charabancs — a Leyland, a Daimler and a pair of AECs, all with bodywork by Kiddle of Bournemouth — entered service in the spring of 1919.

Prior to the new arrivals, on 1 January 1919, the company had moved to larger premises at the Royal Mews in Norwich Avenue, Bournemouth, where ticket and enquiry offices were built. The registered office, since 1916 at the Wilts & Dorset Bank Chambers in Bournemouth, was also moved to Royal Mews.

The company was optimistic of expansion, and the new premises were designed for that growth. This optimism was soon realised, the Bournemouth–Lymington service finally starting in May 1919. It was operated initially in conjunction with Lymington & District Motor Services Co Ltd and had been authorised following the setting of fares within the tram operating area — Bournemouth and Christchurch — 50% higher than those charged by the Corporation. (This was to prove a long-term feature of services operating in the Bournemouth area; buses displayed notices advising passengers that the vehicle was 'Not on Service for Bournemouth Corporation Passengers' right up until October 1986, when deregulation of local services eradicated such agreements.) However, Bournemouth & District had insufficient vehicles to operate the route, and for the first nine months Lymington & District operated alone. The first new service actually operated by Bournemouth & District was from Bournemouth Square to Ringwood and began on Saturday 19 July 1919, using a pair of Daimlers hired in from Aldershot & District. The same month witnessed the delivery of two Leyland 28-seaters with Kiddle bodies. These were joined over the next few months by a further eight Leylands, all with 34-seat Dodson bodywork, and by March 1920 the fleet stood at 14 vehicles.

2. HANTS & DORSET

Of the formative years of Hants & Dorset, 1920 was perhaps the most significant. Although largely forgotten today, Trade Cars of Southampton could be regarded as one of the most significant operators purchased by Bournemouth & District. With this operator came premises at 368 Shirley Road, three buses and private-hire licences. The decision had been made to expand outside Bournemouth, and although the existing company name was suitable for this expansion, it was felt that other towns and cities would prefer to have an operator they could consider their own. Thus vehicles operating from the newly acquired premises bore the fleetname 'Hants & Dorset', and on 27 July 1920 the company's name was officially changed to Hants & Dorset Motor Services Ltd.

In the meantime Thomas Tilling was looking to expand and was busy acquiring an interest in each of the BAT subsidiaries.

Following an investment in the fledgling H&D, Thomas Wolsey joined the Board of Directors to represent the Tilling organisation. With Tilling and BAT happy to invest, expansion continued, and further Dodson-bodied Leylands were received. Licences to operate from Southampton to Lymington and Winchester were obtained, assisted by the purchase of Bunce of Chandlers Ford and its licence to operate the Winchester service. In August a service to Romsey began, followed a little later by another to Bishops Waltham, via Swaythling and Botley, which was extended to Petersfield in 1922. Petersfield became the limit of H&D expansion in this direction.

In November 1922 Portsmouth Corporation granted the necessary licences to enable the company to participate in a Southampton–Portsmouth service via Fareham, jointly with Southdown Motor Services, and the following year a further joint

The precarious nature of the rear entrance would hardly satisfy the authorities today, but Dodson-bodied Leyland G5 single-decker 44 (EL 4574) was the height of modernity when delivered in November 1920. Seen in Petersfield in June 1926, this vehicle was sold for use as a lorry in 1929.
Pamlin Prints / James Prince collection

service, between Portsmouth and Winchester, was introduced. However, by 1924 direct through working between Southampton and Portsmouth had ceased, both companies terminating their journeys at Fareham, although through fares were available, and passengers were able to continue their journey by transferring vehicles. In the same year the Lee-on-the-Solent and Warsash services of Gosport-based Enterprise Services were acquired, along with a mixed bag of 10 vehicles.

Expansion was also continuing around Bournemouth, and licences were awarded to allow the introduction and extension of numerous routes. By 1924 a joint service with Wilts & Dorset was running between Bournemouth and Salisbury, and other routes were running out to Wareham, Shaftesbury and Weymouth.

But Hants & Dorset was not the only operator with an eye to operation in and around Bournemouth. In August 1921 the Elliott brothers, who traded as Royal Blue, had been awarded 12 omnibus licences for services from Bournemouth to Ringwood, Wimborne and Lymington. The Elliotts obtained 14 AEC and Daimler lorries from the War Department and set about rebuilding the incomplete chassis into 12 complete units with new charabanc bodies by Dodson.

Due to family illness the Elliotts' plans were put on hold. However, in 1923 Royal Blue asked for 10 licences. H&D responded by asking for 30, but all 40 were refused. After intense negotiation Royal Blue sold the 12 Daimlers to Hants & Dorset and agreed to give up any interest in operating stage services

around Bournemouth; in return Hants & Dorset agreed not to operate any tours, excursions or long-distance services from the town. This agreement was set to last for 21 years, and the two companies worked happily alongside each other until events just 11 years later resulted in changes that neither could have foreseen.

In July 1924 the fleet was swelled by 10 more buses by the acquisition of Enterprise of Gosport, and services between Lee-on-the-Solent, Sarisbury and Warsash were added to the company's portfolio. Of the acquired vehicles — a mixture of Daimler, Thornycroft and Dennis single-deckers — one was significant. FX 4431 was an AEC Y type with 34-seat open-top double-deck bodywork — the first double-decker operated by Hants & Dorset. Further services and vehicles in the Gosport area were acquired the following September, when H. W. Smith was taken over.

The year 1925 saw the delivery of a number of new vehicles. Nine Leyland SG9 rear-entrance single-deckers with bodywork by either Leyland or Beadle were the first forward-control, half-cab vehicles in the fleet and were followed by half a dozen little (13-seat) Morris chasers, the first vehicles with pneumatic tyres. Meanwhile the first new double-deckers were seven Leyland GH7s with 51-seat open-top, open-staircase bodywork by Brush. By now Leyland was the preferred chassis manufacturer, and further single- and double-deckers of this make were supplied over the next few years.

By now the livery was green, a similar shade to that used by Maidstone & District. The earliest double-deckers were all-over green, while single-deckers featured cream roofs. As was common at the time, elaborate lining-out was employed, and the grand 'HANTS & DORSET' fleetname, in lettering of graduated height, made for a stately appearance.

The livery looked especially fine on the largest single-deckers operated to date. A Leyland 'zoo' was being formed, new single-deck models being named after a creature conveying something of the vehicles' purpose. The first four Lioness single-deckers, which arrived in the spring of 1927, were capable of swallowing up large numbers of passengers, while a pair of little 20-seater Leverets, delivered later in the year, was used to chase after competitors' buses on contested routes. Double-deckers, on the other hand, had mighty, sometimes mythical names to reflect their stature; received soon after the Leverets were four of the grandly named but uncommon Leyland Leviathan. Perhaps the most famous Leyland double-decker, announced in 1927, was the Titan. This, along with the equivalent Tiger single-decker,

was a revolutionary model featuring a low-slung chassis and levels of reliability and refinement unheard of in the motor-bus world.

Hants & Dorset embraced the Titan, buying no fewer than 70 of the initial TD1 model over the next four years. The first were open-toppers with Short or Leyland bodywork, but the 1929 deliveries introduced roofs to double-deckers with a mixture of highbridge and lowbridge types. The lowbridge body was especially useful for increasing route availability, given the area's various low bridges, and to avoid damage from overhanging trees. Single-decker preference leant towards the Lion, which had first entered the fleet in 1926, and more entered service in the ensuing years.

The extra Leylands were used to replace earlier vehicles and to inaugurate new routes. In 1928 permission was granted to start new services within Poole. One route in particular, from Poole to County Gates via Lower Parkstone, brought Hants & Dorset into direct competition with Bournemouth's tramcars, which had been operating into Poole since 1905. The Poole & District Electric

The chain ferry linking the Sandbanks peninsula with Studland, on the Isle of Purbeck, saves around 35 miles from the journey between Bournemouth and Swanage and has for many years been a regular carrier of Hants & Dorset buses and their successors. This view from 1928 shows one of the Leyland Lions, 256 (RU 7561), on the Sandbanks side of the harbour.
British Commercial Vehicle Museum L005361

By 1930 the standard single-decker was a forward-entrance Leyland Lion, complete with roof rack, as depicted here by Leyland's official photographer.
This bus went on to become one of the BB class, some of which lasted until 1950 following rebodying in 1947.
British Commercial Vehicle Museum L006964

A rear view of the same bus, showing the roof rack and the access ladder slung between the offside wheels.
British Commercial Vehicle Museum L006965

9

Tramway Co, a BET subsidiary, had been operating within Poole since 1901 but was not permitted to enter Bournemouth. Bournemouth Corporation did not want the Poole trams in its borough, and a number of battles with BET culminated in the Corporation's starting its own tramway in July 1902. Expansion was swift, and during 1905 BET conceded defeat and indicated a willingness to dispose of Poole & District. However, the councillors in Poole wanted some control over the tramway, and, although Bournemouth took over Poole & District in June 1905, the trackwork was owned by Poole Corporation. A 30-year agreement was reached whereby the Bournemouth tramways leased the track from Poole.

By 1928 the 'Lower Line' in Parkstone was in poor condition, and considerable expenditure would have been needed to bring it up to standard. The efficiency with which Hants & Dorset operated its services had been noticed in council chambers, and,

rather than renew the track, Poole arranged for H&D to replace the tram services with motor buses. The Lower Parkstone tracks were subsequently removed, and travel between Bournemouth and Poole in green Leyland Titans was possible for the first time, though trams still ran through on the Upper Parkstone lines. Interestingly, the Poole Corporation Act of 1928, which authorised the closing of the line, did allow Poole to replace the trams with 'omnibuses moved by electrical power'. If Poole had exercised this right, trolleybuses could have been running in the town before Bournemouth's own system was established, and the story of Hants & Dorset could have been very different.

Meanwhile the practice of expanding by purchasing smaller operators continued. November 1927 saw the acquisition of Greyhound Motor Coaches and the Waterways & Docks Bus Co, both of Southampton, to be followed a year later by an assortment of vehicles from Parsons of Swanage.

3. THE 1930s

The Southern Railway bought an interest in Hants & Dorset in November 1930. Although the Southern had been granted powers to operate buses in 1928, like most other railway companies it decided to buy shares in existing bus companies rather than engage in wasteful competition. This resulted in the acquisition of 33% of Hants & Dorset's shares and details of principal train services appearing in the company's timetables.

The railway's influence could be felt at trade-union level, where the National Union of Railwaymen was chosen to represent the employees' interests rather than the more appropriate T&GWU. Indeed, the Railway, Maritime & Transport Union (RMT) continues to represent a number of staff employed by Hants & Dorset's successors.

On Sunday 8 March 1931 Hants & Dorset and Royal Blue jointly opened an impressive two-tier bus station in the centre of Bournemouth. The building was designed from the outset to be operated jointly by both companies, the coach services and tours of Royal Blue using the lower level and the Hants & Dorset buses the upper. A few months later, in July 1931, a new bus station was opened in Fareham. Although by no means as impressive as that at Bournemouth, it was nonetheless a useful addition to the network. Building work continued during the 1930s, further stations opening at West Marlands Terrace, Southampton, and in The Broadway, Winchester, where the now-famous bus station opened on 20 June 1935.

This may be an opportune moment to have a look at how far Bournemouth & District had grown in the 15 years or so since obtaining the four Straker-Squire charabancs and trying to obtain licences from Bournemouth Corporation. The company timetable for May 1932 details a network of services covering a huge part of Dorset and Hampshire, and a range of local and trunk routes was operated. The Bournemouth–Salisbury service was a good example

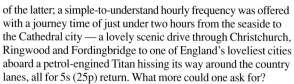

of the latter; a simple-to-understand hourly frequency was offered with a journey time of just under two hours from the seaside to the Cathedral city — a lovely scenic drive through Christchurch, Ringwood and Fordingbridge to one of England's loveliest cities aboard a petrol-engined Titan hissing its way around the country lanes, all for 5s (25p) return. What more could one ask for?

Alternatively, you could save threepence (1¼p) and jump aboard a bus for Shaftesbury. Another lovely drive through Wimborne, Blandford and the Dorset countryside would end with the bus arriving in the charming country town 2hr 5min after leaving Bournemouth's impressive omnibus station.

Of course, in the Bournemouth area there were only a few short-distance routes, as the agreement restricting the carrying of passengers wholly within the borough was in force. The faretables reflect this in not offering fares for any points between the omnibus station and edge of town. In nearby Poole a number of local runs was offered, as no such agreement was in force.

Bournemouth was not the only operational centre. In the east of the area there was a range of services linking Southampton with the many villages nestled in the heart of the New Forest, as well as a variety of major trunk routes linking the city with Eastleigh, Winchester, Fareham and Petersfield.

A quick look at the map of services shows that the company's western and eastern areas were actually quite separate. While services radiating from Bournemouth and Poole went as far east as Lyndhurst, they did not venture any further. Similarly, buses from Southampton would venture westwards but not far enough to rub shoulders with the Bournemouth services. There were, however, two exceptions. Like Bournemouth, Southampton provided a service to Salisbury, deep in Wilts & Dorset territory, and this, like the route from Bournemouth, terminated in Salisbury's unusually named Endless Street. There was also the company's main trunk service linking Bournemouth with Southampton, a mammoth 2hr 45min trek across Hampshire linking numerous towns and villages.

Services were operated by a fleet of 169 green buses, all save half a dozen 20-seat Chevrolet chasers built by Leyland. The oldest vehicles were Lion single-deckers and GH7 open-toppers from 1926. Most of the fleet was now fitted with pneumatic tyres, the GH7s having been so equipped in 1927, and the newer Titans and Lions were some of the most modern vehicles available. More were on order for the following year.

Each new vehicle purchased was allocated either the fleet number left vacant by the bus it was replacing or the next available

even number; odd numbers were still eschewed. By 1930 this system had made vehicle allocation a skilled affair, and fleet-number prefixes were introduced to distinguish vehicle types. Unlike systems used in many other companies, the letters bore no relation to the vehicle make and were allotted alphabetically, the original set of class letters used being as follows:

A	Leyland GH7
B	Leyland Lion PLSC
BB	Leyland Lion LT1
C	Leyland Leviathan
D	Leyland Leveret
E	Leyland Titan
F	Leyland Tiger

G was used in March 1932 for the first Leyland Titan TD2s, which introduced Eastern Counties bodywork to the passengers of Dorset and Hampshire. Eastern Counties' bodybuilding division would be reformed in 1936 as Eastern Coach Works, which from 1939 would go on to supply hundreds of bodies for Hants & Dorset. Delivered alongside the TD2s was a batch of 35-seat Leyland Lion LT5s, known as the BG class.

Meanwhile, Oakleigh Motor Services of Hordle and Billie's Bus Service of Lymington were both acquired in February 1933, bringing a range of services around the Lymington area and a couple of 14-seat buses, a Ford and a further Chevrolet. These lasted little more than a year but still received fleet numbers, the Ford becoming J200 and the Chevrolet H388, both introducing new class letters.

It has to be said that the system could become a little obscure. A year after the G-class Leyland Titan TD2s had been delivered a further batch arrived which, apart from having Brush bodywork, were identical. However, these received M prefixes. The next Titans, which arrived in 1934, were Brush-bodied TD3s forming the A class, following the withdrawal of the last Leyland GH7 earlier in the year. The double-deck fleet was now completely Leyland Titan. Single-deck developments continued with smaller vehicles for lightly trafficked routes, the L-class Leyland Cub arriving in 1933 and the K-class Dennis Ace the following year.

The only trolleybus system to operate within Hants & Dorset territory sparked into life in 1933, when Bournemouth Corporation began a trial to establish whether its tram system could be replaced effectively by trackless trolleys. It was an overwhelming success, and the replacement programme began the following year. The lease on the remaining tram lines within Poole was due to expire two years later, and Bournemouth

A glance inside Fareham depot in 1931 reveals a mixed bag of Leyland buses being attended to by a trio of competent fitters. From left to right are Titan TD1 E238 (TR 5328), Leyland Lion B28 (TR 2623), TD1 E286 (RU 9494), Lion B190 (TR 2837) and Leyland GH7 A158 (RU 2664). E238 would go on to serve Hants & Dorset for a further 20 years, following rebodying by ECW in 1944.
Bristol Vintage Bus Group

Carrying an incorrect registration plate, Leyland-bodied Titan TD1 E290 (TR 7465) splashes through a flash flood on the Southampton– Romsey route. This bus passed to Wilts & Dorset in 1939.
British Commercial Vehicle Museum L007224

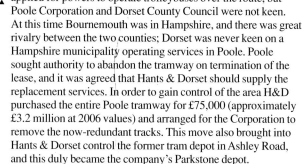

Leyland Lion LT5A BA78 (ALJ 783) of 1935 takes the lead in disembarking from the Sandbanks ferry. Originally fitted with a sliding roof and luggage racks, this Brush-bodied 34-seater would serve Hants & Dorset for 15 years. *British Commercial Vehicle Museum L021595*

applied for powers to operate trolleybuses over the route, but Poole Corporation and Dorset County Council were not keen. At this time Bournemouth was in Hampshire, and there was great rivalry between the two counties; Dorset was never keen on a Hampshire municipality operating services in Poole. Poole sought authority to abandon the tramway on termination of the lease, and it was agreed that Hants & Dorset should supply the replacement services. In order to gain control of the area H&D purchased the entire Poole tramway for £75,000 (approximately £3.2 million at 2006 values) and arranged for the Corporation to remove the now-redundant tracks. This move also brought into Hants & Dorset control the former tram depot in Ashley Road, and this duly became the company's Parkstone depot.

Trams finished in Poole on 7 June 1935. Interestingly, before deciding on replacing trams with trolleybuses, Bournemouth Corporation had been approached by Hants & Dorset with an offer to take over the whole system; had this been accepted, the residents of Bournemouth would never have enjoyed the trolleybus system that served the town so well.

To operate the new services Hants & Dorset purchased a batch of 18 Brush-bodied Leyland Titan TD4c lowbridge double-deckers, with torque converters; as the torque converter dispensed with the usual gearbox and eliminated gear changes, it was considered that these buses would help former tram drivers switch over to driving buses. In the company's idiosyncratic numbering system these fine buses became the P class.

The year 1935 was a hugely significant one in the history of Hants & Dorset. It had opened with the assets of Royal Blue being taken over by Tilling and distributed between Western National, Southern National and H&D. Just under 100 vehicles were involved, 60 coaches being distributed between Southern National and Western National, along with the express-service operation. The excursions and tours operations based in Bournemouth and Southampton became the responsibility of Hants & Dorset, bringing with them the Pavilion Garage in Bournemouth, a garage in Yarmouth, Isle of Wight, and a number of shops and offices. A mixed collection of 38 coaches joined the fleet, including a number of Duple-bodied Daimlers and AEC Regals along with four side-engined AEC Qs which, following a rare moment of logic in the fleet-numbering scheme, became the Q class.

At the same time Tilling was also finalising the purchase of Tourist Motor Coaches, the largest excursion operator in the Southampton area, completed in May 1935. Although having fewer vehicles than Elliott Bros, its two-tone-blue-and-white coaches were often to be seen on extended tours and express services from Southampton to London, Torquay and Liverpool. Tourist was also divided among the three Tilling subsidiaries, 10 Strachans-bodied Leyland Tiger TS2s and a solitary Albion joining the Hants & Dorset fleet, along with premises in Grosvenor Place which were rebuilt into a large bus depot and coach station.

Some of the coaches acquired from Royal Blue were replaced by a batch of brand-new Leyland Tigers with Beadle bodywork, which arrived within weeks of the deal being finalised. These entered service in a blue-and-turquoise livery, suitable for both companies, featuring a new garter scroll fleetname of 'Royal Blue and Tourist'. Further Tigers were delivered in 1936 in the same colours, one of which was bodied by Brush and exhibited at the 1935 Commercial Motor Show. A trio of neat little Leyland Cubs also arrived in 1936 for use on certain extended tours.

A change in policy saw the blue livery replaced by a new scheme of cream with two-tone green but retaining the joint fleetname. A repainting programme was introduced, the blue

A 1935 photograph of Bournemouth Square, taken from atop the bus station, featuring a couple of Sunbeam trolleybuses, an AEC Regent of the Corporation fleet and a line of excursion coaches plying for trade. Heading up this line are Royal Blue AEC Qs LJ 8600 and AEL 2, both shortly to join Hants & Dorset upon the takeover of Royal Blue's Bournemouth operations. *James Prince collection*

Seen waiting patiently on Swanage seafront is Leyland Cub L552 (BLJ 991), earning its keep on the town service, an hourly route linking New Swanage and Herston Cross with Swanage station. New in June 1936, this vehicle was to have a short life with Hants & Dorset, being requisitioned by the War Office in September 1939 and destined never to return. *Andrew N. Porter*

15

A trio of Brush-bodied Titans on layover at Bournemouth. From left to right are TD4 A586 (CRU 704) of 1937, P346 (ARU 166), a TD4c delivered in May 1935, and A190 (ALJ 781), a TD3c which arrived two months earlier. *A. D. Packer*

Time for a quick chat in Christchurch High Street. Brush-bodied Leyland TD4 A560 (BLJ 995) squeezes past Bournemouth Sunbeam MS2 trolleybus 77 (AEL 405) in 1936. *Red House Museum*

being virtually eradicated during the winter of 1936/7. At the same time half-a-dozen AEC Regals from 1935 — the newest vehicles taken over from Royal Blue — and all of the former Tourist Tigers were sent away for rebodying by Beadle. This was the first such exercise undertaken by the company and provided a quicker and cheaper alternative than buying new. Even though the original bodies were fairly recent, the replacements were to be the same style as that on the newly delivered Tigers and projected a very strong, uniform image for the fleet.

Vehicle developments for the bus fleet continued. To provide comparison with the Titans a highbridge Willowbrook-bodied AEC Regent, S516, arrived in 1935. The S prefix was used for vehicles not fitting into the main schemes, such as one-offs or those acquired when taking over other operators. But the Titan was still favourite, and S516 was destined to remain unique.

Further Leyland Titan TD4s arrived during the spring of 1937, but passengers boarding one of these smart new Brush-bodied double-deckers would have been left in no doubt that there was something different under the bonnet. The diesel engine had arrived. Development of the diesel engine — or oil engine, as it was then more commonly known — had progressed greatly during the 1930s, and many operators were switching over, won over by the promise of improved fuel economy and longer engine life.

Admittedly, the very best oil engine of the era could never hope to match the refinement of petrol-engined vehicles, but the die had been cast. A few smaller single-deckers aside, Hants & Dorset would buy no more new petrol-engined vehicles. A programme was put in place to convert the existing Titans to oil, occasionally with Leyland units but more often with the Gardner 5LW. Of the 131 petrol Titans owned, 56 had been converted by the time war was declared, though none of the single-deckers was modified.

Further Beadle-bodied Leyland Tiger coaches were received during January and February 1938, similar to those already in use on tours, but now diesel.

Later in 1938 the first Bristol double-deckers arrived. Full control of Bristol had passed to the Tilling Group in 1935, and, with the launch of the simple but rugged Bristol K and L types at the end of 1937, subsidiaries were encouraged to take Bristol chassis. Often described as a 'busman's bus', the K5G was a 26ft-long double-decker designed primarily around requirements set down by the Tilling companies. Fitted with a Gardner 5LW engine, similar to those currently replacing the petrol engines in the company's Titans, the first batch of 23 had Brush lowbridge bodywork seating 54. Next to arrive were the first examples of the L type (the K's single-deck equivalent), fitted with Beadle bus bodywork featuring a forward entrance and a sliding roof.

A further batch of single-deckers arrived in the spring of 1939. The second vehicle in this group, CCR 855 was the very first Hants & Dorset bus to be issued with an odd fleetnumber — TS701. The policy of reissuing the numbers of departing buses to new vehicles had ceased in 1937, and from now on new deliveries would be numbered in order, with odd and even numbers. However, the allocation of class letters continued, and the new Bristol range was given T-series numbers — TD for the double-deck Ks and TS for the Ls.

Another milestone was reached with the delivery of Bristol K TD709, Hants & Dorset's first ECW-bodied bus. What was to be the standard combination of Bristol chassis and ECW body had arrived, to be followed by more than 1,300 over the next 43 years.

For a while after the takeover of Royal Blue and Tourist new coaches were delivered in blue with joint Hants & Dorset, Royal Blue and Tourist fleetnames. Showing the short-lived scheme is 1936 Beadle-bodied Leyland Cub L452 (CEL 223).
British Commercial Vehicle Museum L018750

In contrast, similar Cub L740 (CCR 856) of 1939 displays the new livery of green and cream while retaining the joint fleetname. In 1950 L740 would be rebuilt as a service bus with an air-operated entrance door fitted in the bay behind the original hinged door and a relocated fuel tank, the fitting of a diesel engine in 1953 completing the transformation.
Nellie G. Smith

▲ Posing majestically for the official photographer is TD717 (ERU 593), a member of the first batch of ECW-bodied Bristol K5Gs. Delivered early in 1939, it would be renumbered 1042 in 1950, remaining in service (like many of its type) until 1959. *Ian Allan Library*

4. WAR

At the outbreak of World War 2 the fleet stood at 311 — almost double that of just seven years earlier. Just over half of these were double-deckers, ranging from 1928-vintage Leyland TD1 open-toppers through to the ECW-bodied Ks. Of the single-deckers, 80 were buses and 68 coaches, the eldest of these being 1929 Leyland Lions.

Almost immediately, 19 vehicles — five Leyland Cub buses and, a little later, the entire batch of 1935 Leyland Tiger coaches — were requisitioned by the War Office. Of these, only three Tigers would return after the war. Coaches quickly became superfluous as all excursions and tours, along with certain lightly used bus services, were suspended following the declaration of hostilities.

Throughout 1939 company staff had been enlisting in the Air Raid Precaution units, and, to reduce visibility from the air, new regulations came into force limiting the lighting of vehicles at night. Initially, headlights were simply bent down on their brackets to restrict the upward glare. Although it had been decided to suspend all bus services in Hampshire one hour after sunset, those in Dorset continued to run as normal, and the restricted lighting made driving treacherous for both the drivers and pedestrians. It was quickly decided to straighten the headlights but remove the nearside bulb and mask the offside lamp. This was better, but the problem was not completely solved until slotted hoods were fitted to both lamps.

Internal lighting was also restricted, initially by applying blue lacquer to the windows; this may have been a solution for reducing the emission of light during darkness, but it made for very unpleasant journeying during daytime. Again, a solution was found whereby most light bulbs were removed and the remainder painted with the same blue lacquer. As an additional aid, conductors were issued with small torches which could be attached to their shoulder straps.

Externally, white paint markings were applied to mudguards, dumb-irons and wheel arches, to improve the visibility of the bus at night from the ground, while the process began of painting the cream roofs grey, to reduce the visibility of the buses from the air. Although none of the company's premises was seriously damaged during the war, at the beginning of hostilities the threat was very real, and in an attempt to reduce the risk of losing vehicles staff were encouraged to take buses home and park them up on side streets.

For nine months from October 1940 Hants & Dorset was one of many operators sending vehicles to London to help replace vehicles lost in the blitz, despatching 13 Titans. London was already desperate for vehicles, and the arrival of buses from operators around the country proved to be a great morale boost for Londoners, reassuring them that they were not alone in their hour of need.

But 1940 also saw deliveries of further new vehicles. These had been ordered during the early part of 1939 and were to normal specification. They included the last Beadle-bodied Bristol L buses. Across the country, manufacture of buses was curtailed as the emphasis switched to producing vehicles and aircraft for the war effort. The Ministry of Supply became responsible for ensuring that the country's manufacturing resources were used as effectively as possible and, working with the Ministry of Transport, placed severe restrictions on bus operators. The sale of vehicles, both new and second-hand, was strictly controlled, and operators were unable to make any fleet changes without permission. This meant that many of the older vehicles would have to continue longer than originally envisaged, and a rebuilding programme was introduced. Many of the 1933 Titans were rebuilt by Beadle, with little visible alteration, while ECW

▲ It's the middle of the war, and weary-looking Titan P368 (ARU 167) is seen in full Blackout guise, complete with headlamp masks and white edging to the wheel arches. One of the gearless TD4c models purchased for the Poole tram-replacement services in 1935, it was by now based at Southampton. *W. J. Haynes*

was contracted to refurbish some of the 1935 TD3s, again with little change to the overall appearance.

By 1942 operators were clamouring for new vehicles, and the utility bus was announced. Officially known as the Standard Wartime Specification for Double-deckers, the utility was built to a strict design, with basic features reflecting the raw materials and level of skilled workers available, which resulted in a bus which was both spartan and angular. Vehicles were allocated by the Ministry with little regard to existing company policy.

Hants & Dorset was fairly lucky with its initial allocation — four Bristol Ks, which arrived in 1942. However a limited number of manufacturers was used, not including ECW, so they were fitted with bodywork by Strachans or Duple, the first double-deckers from these builders. The chassis were 'unfrozen', constructed from parts on which work had stopped following the outbreak of war. Further Strachans-bodied Bristol Ks would arrive in 1944 and 1945.

The next utilities were not unfrozen, and one can imagine the cool reception which greeted their arrival. Guy Motors had been selected as the main supplier of bus chassis during the war, and its Arab model appeared in the most unlikely of places. Nine Gardner-engined Arabs, CD950-8, were delivered with a mixture of Strachans, Brush and Roe bodywork.

Even in the darkest days of the war changes were taking place that would affect the company for many years. The two constituents of H&D's parent company, Tilling & BET, had never really hit it off, and it was decided to close down the T&BAT combine, dividing the interests between Tilling Motor Services Ltd and BET Omnibus Services Ltd. In September 1942 Hants & Dorset became a Tilling company.

But the war rumbled on. More than 60 years later it is almost impossible to appreciate the effect the war had on everyone's daily life. Being a large port, Southampton suffered badly from large-scale air raids. There were 57 attacks in all, with more than 1,300 bombs and 30,000 incendiary devices dropped. More than 600 civilians were killed, and nearly 45,000 buildings damaged or destroyed. Incredibly, there were reports that the glow of Southampton burning could be seen from as far away as Cherbourg.

Bournemouth, meanwhile, was being utilised as a garrison town, providing training, leave facilities and accommodation for visiting Allied Forces, and was particularly full with American, British and Canadian forces in the period leading up to D-Day. The section of the coast to the east and west of the town was very important, Poole Harbour being the departure-point for many ships participating in the D-Day landings.

Bournemouth itself was not usually a main target of the Luftwaffe but was on the route for other targets, such as Coventry, and bombers were known to unload their unused bombs on the town. In all, 219 local people were killed by bombing during the war, the worst attack occurring on the morning of Sunday 23 May 1943: Holdenhurst Road, near the Central railway station, was badly damaged, while several large buildings around the town were destroyed; one device landed adjacent to the bus station, blowing out the windows of 25 buses. It was some time before repairs were completed, buses running in service for the next few days with missing windows and sacking in place to keep out the worst of the draughts. The only Hants & Dorset buses completely destroyed during the war were a 1932 Titan and an 11-month-old Bristol L5G, both lost during a raid on Gosport during January 1941.

During 1944 some stability returned. The aerial bombardment had ceased, and the Blackout restrictions were no longer enforced as rigidly as they had been. Gradually the buses regained their cream roofs, and services slowly returned to peacetime levels.

June 1945 saw the retirement of William Wells Graham, Hants & Dorset's founder and General Manager. He had seen the company grow to one with almost 350 vehicles and controlling a large area of both Dorset and Hampshire, and towards the end of his working life he quite frequently expressed the opinion that perhaps the company had grown a little too big, being disappointed that the days when he knew every member of staff on sight had gone. Awarded the OBE in the New Year's Honours list of 1942, he enjoyed only a short retirement and died peacefully in May 1947.

5. PEACE RETURNS

As the war neared its conclusion the company started to review the position of its fleet. At the beginning of 1945 there were 332 vehicles, the oldest of which were the 1928 Titans. These had also been the oldest vehicles at the beginning of the war but had undergone a metamorphosis during 1943. The rebuilding exercise undertaken on certain vehicles earlier in the war had proved successful and was extended to the oldest buses. Unsurprisingly, it was not considered worthwhile simply to rebuild the open-top bodies, so each chassis, having had its original body removed at Southampton, was driven the 210 miles to Lowestoft for ECW to fit a brand-new, covered-top lowbridge version. Although the petrol engines were still hissing and burbling under the bonnet, the new bodywork gave these veterans a new lease of life, and the last example was not withdrawn until July 1951.

The prewar level of fleet replacement had been suspended during the war, and, although rebuilding and rebodying helped, the effect of increasing passenger numbers and a fleet in need of modernisation meant that extra vehicles were needed urgently. Orders were placed for new buses, but there were still severe restrictions on supply, and it was to be a few years before deliveries reached an acceptable level.

As a short-term measure the first second-hand buses, apart from those acquired when taking over operators, entered the fleet. Brighton, Hove & District supplied three AEC Regents, built in 1932 (a time when the Brighton fleet was closely associated with Thomas Tilling in London) and fitted with Gardner oil engines in 1937. The first for Hants & Dorset since the experimental Willowbrook-bodied example of 1935, they were repainted in a non-standard green-and-white livery, without fleetnames, before entering service. Fleet numbers were allocated in the oddball S series, and they lasted until the fleet situation improved, not being sold until 1949.

But new vehicles did arrive in 1946 — not many, but new nonetheless. Eight Bristol Ks, all with ECW bodies, in what was to become the classic livery of Tilling green with two cream bands, signalled the start of postwar recovery. These were the first Bristols in the fleet with the new lower PV2-type radiator, which greatly improved the type's appearance. Bodywork was to

ECW's standard early-postwar pattern with sliding side vents mounted separately above the windows. One of the batch (TD783) was a K6B, the first Bristol-engined bus for the fleet, with a six-cylinder, 8.1-litre AVW unit; the rest were K5Gs with the usual Gardner 5LW.

Slowly things got back to normal. A small excursion programme started in April 1946, and tours of the Isle of Wight recommenced the following year. Three years later Southern Vectis agreed to undertake these tours on a contract basis, so that the Yarmouth garage taken over from Elliott Bros could be closed.

In 1947 an influx of new buses and coaches showed that delivery levels were starting to improve. The six-cylinder Gardner 6LW engine was introduced to the company in a batch of Beadle-bodied Bristol L6G coaches, soon followed by similar machines equipped with either Beadle or, unusually, Dutfield bodywork. Beadle also supplied new bodywork for eight elderly Leyland Lions.

◄ Doing a remarkable impersonation of a London Tilling ST type is ex-Brighton, Hove & District AEC Regent S517 (GW 6279), seen in Southampton during 1948. One of three acquired in 1945, this bus was built in 1932, at a time when the Brighton fleet was closely associated with Thomas Tilling in London, explaining the London-issued registration numbers.
courtesy Office of Public Sector Information

Grosvenor Square depot at Southampton was an impressive structure and worthy of record by the official photographer in May 1946. Neatly assembled are eight double-deckers representing the major types operated, the Leyland Titan being represented by the three TD4c models and a TD3c peeking out of the right-hand doorway, while the left-hand door is blocked by a quartet of Bristol K5Gs, three with ECW bodywork and a solitary example with Brush. *Ian Allan Library*

August saw the arrival of the first of two dozen K5Gs. These had an updated version of the ECW body incorporating slightly recessed windows with neatly rounded corners and sliding ventilators incorporated into the main frame. Painted in the new livery, these were truly classic buses. If that were not enough, the arrival of six ECW-bodied L5Gs helped to modernise the single-deck bus fleet.

Alongside this investment the rebodying programme was accelerated, further Titans being sent for attention by either ECW or Beadle, along with one or two of the earliest L5G saloons. Perhaps surprisingly, new Leyland Titans also appeared, seven PD1As, carrying lowbridge ECW bodywork similar to that on the K5Gs and given appropriate PD959-65 fleet numbers, adding variety to the fleet early in 1948.

However, six years of war had left the country tired, and the surprise election of a Labour Government in 1945 set in motion a further chain of events that would directly affect almost the whole of the country's transport industry. The early postwar years were to prove difficult for bus operators up and down the country,

a combination of continued petrol rationing for private motorists (not lifted until May 1950) and a desire to get out and about following the dark days of the war meaning that the battle-weary fleets of hard-pressed operators were more than ever in demand.

Also popular were the railways, but World War 2 had had a serious impact on their finances, and the new Labour Government came to power with a mandate for change. King George VI's speech to the 1946/7 Parliamentary session announced plans for the nationalisation of the country's transport system. This manifested itself as the 1947 Transport Act, and on 1 January 1948 the railways, canals and road freight transport came under the control of the newly formed, state-owned British Transport Commission (BTC). A new London Transport Executive was also created within this body to replace the London Passenger Transport Board, which had been under Government control since 1939.

The upshot for Hants & Dorset was that the one-third shareholding previously held by the Southern Railway was now state property. Many of the Tilling subsidiaries were in a similar

Dutfield-bodied Bristol Ls were unique to Hants & Dorset. Looking resplendent in the postwar coaching livery of two-tone-green and cream is 656 (HRU 454). *Bristol Vintage Bus Group*

The early postwar years saw a number of non-standard vehicles entering the fleet, including 1146 (GLJ 958), an ECW-bodied Leyland Titan PD1A, delivered in 1948 as PD960. *Ian Allan Library*

Not long to go now for 946 (TK 7285), resting in Woolston yard shortly before withdrawal in 1954. The Leyland Titan TD2 chassis had been new in 1932 with an Eastern Counties body, the oil engine replacing the original petrol unit in 1936, and a new ECW body being fitted 10 years later. *James Prince collection*

The only utility Brush-bodied Guy Arab was despatched to Reading of Portsmouth in 1948 for a body rebuild. Utilities suffered from structural problems due to the poor quality of materials used, particularly unseasoned timber framing. The rubber-mounted windows and altered front end of 1101 (DCR 865), seen at Southampton's Grosvenor Square depot in the early 1950s, reveal that considerable work has been carried out. *Bristol Vintage Bus Group*

The Bell Inn at Rainham, Essex, forms the backdrop for new Bristol K6A TD883 (HLJ 32), with LT roundel on the radiator and no fleetnames, helping out on London Transport route 87 to Gidea Park in 1949. *James Prince collection*

Also helping London Transport, but on Country Area route 336 from Chesham to Watford, on which its green livery would be less out of place, is TD894 (HLJ 43). *Ian Allan Library*

position, and whereas BET, Tilling's former partner in the T&BAT combine, was fiercely opposed to any form of nationalisation, the Board of Tilling took a more pragmatic view and considered their options. This resulted in the BTC's taking over the entire share capital in September 1948, but with the Tilling Association, formed before 1948, acting as a central organisation for procurement, publicity and purchasing.

Hants & Dorset was now a fully nationalised BTC company, although the passenger boarding the green bus in Southampton, Lyndhurst, Poole or Bournemouth would have noticed very little difference. But being part of the new organisation soon meant

that a number of operators were called to assist their new big brother. London Transport was now operating a worn-out fleet. Coupled with the demand for its services and the slow delivery of new vehicles, this meant that vehicle shortages were reaching crisis point. BTC members were persuaded to assist, and it was agreed that between 20% and 25% of new vehicles on order for provincial fleets should be diverted, temporarily, to London. Hants & Dorset had on order a large number of AEC-engined Bristol K6As (six of which had arrived in May 1948), and 39 of these ended up working in London. All were delivered direct to London Transport from the bodybuilders in standard

Tilling green but without fleetnames, the first entering service in September 1948.

Hants & Dorset and others were a little peeved at being expected to give up their own brand-new buses to help out an operator that many felt was a victim of circumstances of its own making. The new vehicles entering service in London had been ordered to replace time-expired buses elsewhere, which meant that many of the vehicle shortages were simply transferred to other operators, and alternative vehicles had to be sourced. First to arrive at Hants & Dorset were six Leyland Titan PD2s built for export to South Africa. These handsome buses, fitted with

Leyland's own bodywork, were the first new highbridge buses since the Short-bodied Titans of 1929 and ended up spending most of their lives on the Southampton–Fawley routes. The arrival of half a dozen Northern Counties-bodied AEC Regents in May 1949 signalled another diverted order. These carried useful lowbridge bodies and had been intended for Western SMT.

More unusual vehicles, ordered to replace earlier vehicles rather than make up for missing Bristols, were a batch of Beadle bus-bodied Bedford OBs, which arrived alongside the Regents. Three more OBs — coaches with classic Duple bodywork — arrived the following year, the last petrol-engined vehicles bought.

The Bristol K with lowbridge ECW body quickly became the postwar standard vehicle,
and 1276 (KEL 719), loading at Eastleigh, represents the KS6B Bristol-engined version.
New in 1950, it would not be withdrawn until 1971. The cab sun visor was a non-standard fitting
specified by Hants & Dorset. *S. J. Butler collection*

6. THE 1950s

Gradually things got back to normal. The buses helping out in London had all returned by April 1950, and new deliveries finally reached acceptable levels. A major event of 1950 was the complete renumbering of the fleet, the first sign being the issuing of non-prefix numbers to the Titans, Regents and Bedfords.

The new system dispensed with codes; each vehicle was now issued with a completely new number in a specific block. Small-capacity single-deckers were numbered between 550 and 599, coaches from 600 onwards, single-deck buses from 700 and double-deckers from 900. Numbers were allocated to vehicles in age order, with no differentiation between the chassis types.

Shaded gold numerals used in the old system were replaced by small cast-metal plates painted black, with the raised numerals left unpainted. To indicate to which depot each vehicle was allocated a second, smaller plate was fitted above the fleet number, coloured according to depot. (In 1956 this would be replaced by colouring the main fleet-number plate, a combination of black, white or yellow numerals on a coloured background — white, blue, black, pink, orange, yellow, green or grey — being used; Poole buses, for example, carried a blue plate with black numerals, while those starting out from Woolston every morning had black plates with yellow numerals.)

The first highbridge Bristol KSWs arrived towards the end of 1951 and were used almost exclusively on the Bournemouth–Poole trunk routes, on which overhead obstructions were not a problem. Standing patiently at Bournemouth is 1311 (KRU 977) ready for service 3, which reached Poole by way of Upper Parkstone. *Bristol Vintage Bus Group*

The Bristol Lodekka revolutionised the concept of the low-height double-decker. Offering a low overall height but with central gangways on both decks, the type became a common sight throughout the Tilling empire. Prototype 1337 (LRU 67) is seen before delivery in April 1953. *S. J. Butler collection*

Vehicle deliveries now became fairly predictable. The double-decker requirement was met by the good old Bristol K, Bristol-engined versions joining the AECs and Gardners from 1950. The slightly longer KS type made its debut in the autumn of that year, to be followed six months later by the 8ft-wide KSW. Aside from the Titans diverted from South Africa in 1948 the entire fleet was of lowbridge layout, but this changed at the end of 1951, when a switch was made to highbridge KSWs, truly impressive-looking vehicles.

Delivered in May 1953, 1336 (LRU 65) was the 298th and last Bristol K bought new, for taken into stock the previous month was 1337 (LRU 67), the company's first Bristol Lodekka. This was a revolutionary design that managed to retain the overall height of a lowbridge bus while using the more convenient highbridge seating layout, with central gangways on both decks. This was achieved mainly by the adoption of a drop-centre rear axle, which enabled the lower-saloon gangway to be on the same level as the platform. More Lodekkas arrived in 1954, but with a mixture of Bristol or Gardner engines (1337 having been a Bristol-engined LD6B model) and featuring green leather seating (rather than moquette), which became standard for double-deckers for the next 13 years. Some also had platform doors, the first for the fleet.

Very few single-deck buses were delivered during the 1950s. The first to enter service during the decade were a pair of unusual Beadle integral buses based on Morris Commercial running units and fitted with 35-seat rear-entrance bodywork. They remained unique within the fleet and were based at Winchester for use on the Salisbury service. More acceptable was the Bristol L. At the very end of 1949 the first of what was to be a fleet of 38 coaches appeared. Initially a batch of six Portsmouth Aviation-bodied rear-entrance coaches with AEC engines arrived, followed soon afterwards by similar vehicles but with Gardner engines and forward entrances. They were equipped with wind-down windows and sumptuous coach seating for use on the growing programme of extended tours.

As 1951 opened a pair of Portsmouth Aviation-bodied dual-purpose coaches had recently been delivered and a further example was on order. The two already in stock were 30ft-long LL6Gs, which had reverted to rear-entrance layout and were the longest vehicles in the fleet. March saw the trio completed with the receipt of a similar but wider coach — the company's first 8ft-wide vehicle.

The Bristol L was popular both as a bus and as a coach and spawned many variants. However, 781 (KLJ 751), with dual-purpose Portsmouth Aviation body, was unique in being the only LWL6G built for the UK.
Bristol Vintage Bus Group

Keeping warm in Winchester in January 1964 is Portsmouth Aviation-bodied Bristol LL6G 780 (KLJ 750), one of two long L types delivered in 1950. Regarded as dual-purpose vehicles, both had their original coach livery replaced by bus colours in 1954 but continued to provide comfortable transport around the Hampshire countryside until withdrawn in 1965. Happily 779 is now preserved.
M. A. Penn

Full fronts, wind-down windows, sliding roofs and just the right amount of chrome added a certain elegance to the 11 ECW-bodied Bristol Ls delivered in 1951. The first coaches delivered in the all-cream livery, they were known as 'Queen Marys'. Carrying 8ft-wide bodies, five, including 692 (KEL 735), were based on the 7ft 6in-wide LL6B chassis, the remainder on the wider LWL6B. *S. J. Butler collection*

The last Bristol Ls were seven LL6Bs delivered in 1952, with rear-entrance ECW 39-seat bodies. Seen in Salisbury when new is 784 (KRU 990), with the original style of fleet-number plate introduced with the 1950 renumbering.
Bristol Vintage Bus Group

◄ In 1953 the company took delivery of its first Bristol LS vehicles, taking advantage of the type's underfloor engine to employ a dual-door layout. All of the bus versions bought new were so fitted, but all were soon altered to front-entrance/exit one-man operation, 793 (NRU 6), seen here at Bournemouth, being dealt with in 1959. *A. D. Packer*

▼ The date is Friday 12 December 1969, and single-door conversion LS5G 794 (NRU 7), having completed the 50min journey from Wimborne Minster, carefully unloads Christmas shoppers in the layover park at Bournemouth bus station. *Alan O. Watkins*

ECW was favoured for the next coaches and supplied 11 35-seat luxury bodies with forward entrances, full fronts, winding windows and sliding roofs. These were the first vehicles delivered in the new coach livery of cream relieved by light-green wheels and wings; interestingly, while all were built to 8ft width, only the last six were built on Bristol LWL chassis, the first five being on the 7ft 6in-wide LL type. All had Bristol engines. The final members of the Bristol L family, which were also bodied by ECW, were 39-seat rear-entrance buses.

The first underfloor-engined buses arrived in February 1953, a pair of Bristol LS5Gs. These had an entrance in the rear overhang and exit alongside the driver, seen as a way of speeding up loading at stops. This was not an uncommon arrangement in Hampshire, the primrose buses and trolleybuses of Bournemouth having standardised on such a system since the early 1930s. A total of 20 dual-door LS buses was delivered, including a pair with coach seating. But by 1958 the increasing amount of one-man operation meant that they all went through the workshops for rebuilding into more conventional front-entrance buses. The LS was also chosen as the basis for the coach fleet, and 19 were taken into stock.

A pair of bizarre-looking tree-loppers were created in 1950 from two Dennis Aces. Built and registered for Southern National, K598 (CTA 519) was diverted to Hants & Dorset when new in 1937. Now numbered 561, this unusual vehicle would remain busy pruning the New Forest foliage until withdrawal in 1965. *Bristol Vintage Bus Group*

Originally fitted with 28 reclining seats, Bristol LS6G 853 (MLJ 148) was one of the first underfloor-engined vehicles delivered to the company and helped to transform the coach fleet. These smart but understated vehicles rendered the front-engined fleet obsolete within a couple of years. Converted for bus work in 1965, 853 would be sold in 1972. *Bristol Vintage Bus Group*

It was at this time that Hants & Dorset became renowned for extending the lives of vehicles and changing the roles of others by embarking upon some quite drastic rebuilding projects. The wartime and postwar rebuilds have already been mentioned, but the 1950s saw further examples of the engineering department's ingenuity. A number of prewar ECW-bodied K5Gs were modernised with the low PV2 radiator and reprofiled front ends, complete with new destination equipment. One of these, 1068, was selected as the prototype for the Cave-Brown-Cave heating/ventilation system which later became familiar on Bristol Lodekkas. This was handy, as Prof T. R. Cave-Brown-Cave was from Southampton University. In 1955 this bus was also fitted with a supercharger, which resulted in the fitting of a Lodekka-style bonnet to accommodate the equipment.

Rebodying had also restarted in 1949. A mixture of Bristol L and K types and some Leyland Titans received new ECW bodies, while three of the 1935 Leyland Tiger coaches — the only vehicles returned by the War Department following requisition — were fitted with new rear-entrance coach-seated Portsmouth Aviation bodies, in bus livery despite their accoutrements.

The original, high-mounted radiator of 1938 Brush-bodied Bristol K5G 1033 (JT 9361) gives the bus a rugged look, capable of handling anything that is thrown at it, including a relaxing run out to Emery Down. In 1954 this bus would be despatched to Lowestoft for rebodying, emerging with a new highbridge ECW body that would extend its life to 1962. *W. Windebank*

Three of the 1938 Beadle-bodied Bristol L5Gs await withdrawal in 1953. No 734 in the centre was one of the type to have been rebuilt with a full canopy, allowing more suitable destination equipment; 729 (BOW 162), on the far right, was converted as a recovery wagon during 1954 and is now preserved as part of the Bournemouth Heritage Collection. *A. D. Packer*

An unusual view of Bristol K5G guinea-pig 1068 (APR 423) shortly after this bus was fitted with the Cave-Brown-Cave heating/ventilation system. At the same time it gained a more upright front end, with a lower PV2 bonnet and deeper cab window, the conventional radiator being rendered superfluous. *A. D. Packer*

▶

Looking modern alongside its contemporaries, 1068 was further modified in 1955 by the fitting of a supercharger which necessitated a wider Lodekka-style bonnet. Sharing the limelight are 1053 (AFX 750), with a much-rebuilt ECW body, and 1076 (APR 431), which has been left in more-or-less original condition.
Ian Allan Library

▼

The Covrad replacement Leyland radiator jars slightly with the modern styling of the ECW body fitted in 1949 to replace the Brush original to 1933 Titan TD2 964 (LJ 7094). Rebodying allowed this veteran to potter around Hampshire for a further five years. *A. D. Packer*

In addition to supplying a number of coaches, Portsmouth Aviation was contracted to fit new dual-purpose bodies to the three Leyland Tigers that had spent eight years with the War Department. June 1955 finds 727 (ARU 182) on a private hire for a rowing club, the temporary fitting of a suitable roof-rack being a useful feature. *A. D. Packer*

Pictured in Southampton in 1958, 1038 (ERU 589), an ECW-bodied Bristol K5G, illustrates the lengths to which Hants & Dorset would go to rebuild vehicles for further use. Entering the workshops in 1951, it emerged with rubber glazing, sliding window vents and new destination screens, enabling it to work through to its 20th birthday in 1959. *Solent Transport Trust*

The open-top rebuilds were distinctive vehicles and served the tourist spots of Dorset and Hampshire for many years. Most were Bristol Ks, but this is the prototype, Leyland Titan TD4 1005 (CRU 701). Pictured in Bournemouth, it was to see service for only one season (1952) as an open-topper, its body being transferred in February 1953 to Bristol K6A 1112 (FRU 309).
British Commercial Vehicle Museum L044972

Further open-toppers entered service in 1953, similar to those of the previous year but of five-bay construction. In 1957 the body fitted to 1944 K6A 1011 was transferred to newer K5G 1143 (GLJ 986), the resultant combination being seen at Bournemouth in July 1962 displaying blinds for the open-toppers' usual haunt, route 6 to Sandbanks.
Terry Williams

From the rear the open-toppers looked fairly conventional. The slot in the rear bulkhead was for the depositing of used tickets which would end up under the rear seat; only by lifting this seat could the area be cleared. Seen at Bournemouth in June 1968, with the body from 1012 (BTR 302), is 1128 (GLJ 971). *David Fereday Glenn*

The appointment in 1949 of Mr G. H. Napthine (from Westcliff-on-Sea Motor Services) as General Manager set in motion the idea of running open-top leisure services, and one of the 1937 Brush-bodied Titans (CRU 701) was chosen as a prototype for conversion. The extensive rebuild resulted in a full-fronted 57-seat open-topper in cream coach livery with green wings. A further six conversions entered service in the spring of 1952, although, after problems with the full-front cab and concealed radiator on the Titan, Strachans utility-bodied Bristols (due for rebuilding anyway) were selected for the treatment. From the outside they were almost indistinguishable from the Leyland. In 1953 five 1938 Brush-bodied K5Gs were converted, these being similar in appearance to the earlier vehicles, albeit of five-bay (rather than six-bay) construction and featuring a row of 'standee' windows above the main window frames. They entered service in time for the 1953 season, along with a further Bristol which had been fitted with the prototype body from the Titan.

To augment the open-top fleet half-a-dozen elderly Ks were rebodied by ECW in 1954 as 8ft-wide convertibles. Keeping an eye on the photographer, the driver of cream-liveried 1034 (ERU 262) takes a quick break at Sandbanks before another run on the 32. *A. D. Packer*

One of the first half-cab coaches adapted for one-man operation was 657 (HRU 455), one of the rare Dutfield-bodied L6Bs, seen in the yard outside Lymington Town station on 4 August 1962. Now full-fronted, it has had its internal bulkhead cut down (to aid fare collection) and a power-operated bus door fitted. The application of bus livery completes the transformation. *Terry Williams*

More open-toppers were obtained during 1954, when 10 prewar Bristol K5Gs went to ECW for fitting with four-bay KSW-style highbridge bodies, six of which were convertible open-toppers. Some of their original bodies were remounted on other chassis, signalling the start of large-scale body swapping which was to affect a number of K types, and in 1957 five of the later open-top bodies were fitted to some of the 1947 ECW-bodied Ks.

Now it was the turn of the single-deckers. At the end of 1956 one of the six-year-old Portsmouth Aviation-bodied Bristol L6Gs emerged from the bodyshops transformed from a 28-seat half-cab coach to a 29-seat full-fronted bus. The original, sumptuous coach seats had been replaced by bus seats taken from withdrawn vehicles, and a luggage rack fitted behind the entrance door, which itself had been replaced by a power-operated jack-knife unit. A bus-style blind display was fitted at the front, and the sliding roof had been replaced by fixed panelling. All this work was intended to make the now rather old fashioned coach into a practical one-man-operated bus. To achieve this the internal bulkhead windows were removed, and ticket-issuing equipment was fitted over the bonnet. The conversion was deemed a success, and further work was undertaken on another four vehicles, including two which were converted from rear-entrance layout. The remaining Bristol L coaches were to undergo a more extreme metamorphosis; by the summer of 1962 these L6Gs had returned from ECW as LL6Bs, with extended chassis and new bodies, their original Gardner engines being exchanged for the Bristol units in some of the earliest Lodekkas.

The 1959 rebuilding of Bournemouth bus and coach station was a major exercise and involved a number of changes, not least the new office block and altered arrangements for vehicles entering and leaving the lower level. Published at the time of opening, these interesting plans show the new layout.
Ian Allan Library

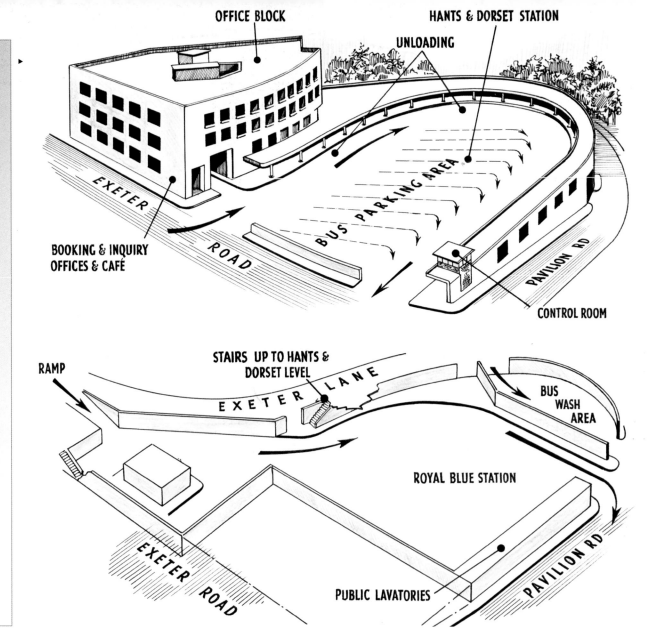

OFFICE BLOCK

HANTS & DORSET STATION

UNLOADING

EXETER ROAD

BUS PARKING AREA

PAVILION RD

BOOKING & INQUIRY OFFICES & CAFÉ

CONTROL ROOM

RAMP

STAIRS UP TO HANTS & DORSET LEVEL

EXETER LANE

BUS WASH AREA

ROYAL BLUE STATION

EXETER ROAD

PUBLIC LAVATORIES

PAVILION RD

In September 1958 Parkstone depot, which used black fleetnumber plates and white numerals, became the Western Area works, its operational vehicles being transferred to Poole. The Eastern Area works were under the same roof as Southampton depot at Grosvenor Square, while the Central Engineering Department was located in nearby Shirley Road. The body works were at Winchester Road, Southampton. An obscure way of identifying whether a bus hailed from the Western or Eastern area (apart from learning all the fleet-number colour combinations) was to look at the tyres — Western buses had Dunlops, Eastern Firestones.

The inflationary spiral, with the price of fuel rising and fares increasing to cover the cost, had got going by the start of the 1950s. Passenger numbers peaked in the early 1950s, after which a gradual but perceptible decline set in. Travelling habits were beginning to change, as people chose to stay at home and watch television rather than catch a bus to the pictures, and days out by bus were replaced by days out by the newly acquired car. In years to come attempts to manage the decline would see alterations to services and an increase in one-man operation. Lower levels of passengers meant less revenue, and the easiest course of action was to reduce services and raise fares, driving away more passengers — a vicious circle. It was a nationwide trend which would continue until at least the late 1990s, by which time there were signs that the decline was beginning to halt.

A couple of smaller Hampshire operators gave up the fight and decided to concentrate on coach hires and excursions. In 1952 Hants & Dorset acquired Easson's Woolston–Hedge End route, followed in 1955 by the Farley, Southampton and Winchester services of Hursley Motor Services, while in 1959 Dorset operator Bere Regis & District relinquished four routes serving the Poole, Bere Regis and Dorchester area. No vehicles were acquired with these takeovers.

The 1950s were not all doom and gloom, for the decline in passenger numbers was not really acknowledged until later in the decade, and a number of construction projects were undertaken to improve the facilities for both the travelling public and staff. Over the winter of 1953/4 the rather cramped facilities in Fareham were enlarged by taking in much of the land formerly occupied by an adjacent chapel. Meanwhile, in Bournemouth, work was about to begin on the bus station. The local fleet was housed and maintained in three separate locations — St Michael's Road, Norwich Avenue and the former Royal Blue Pavilion Garage in Bath Road. The objective was to park the entire allocation at an

enlarged bus station and build a brand-new office block to accommodate the company's head office, until then located on separate sites at the Pavilion Garage and Norwich Avenue. Construction started in March 1957 and succeeded in providing the new office accommodation, along with improved marshalling and control areas designed for one-way traffic flow, maximising the available space. Officially opened on 12 March 1959, the rebuilt lower level boasted new washing and fuelling facilities along with an enlarged Royal Blue coach station, which by now was being used by as many as 18,000 passengers each day. Both the original Royal Mews premises in Norwich Avenue and the St Michael's Road facilities were vacated. The Pavilion garage was retained, mainly for winter storage of coaches and open-top buses.

Underneath the bus station were fuelling and washing facilities. Lodekka 1410 (XEL 544) is seen specially posed beneath the drop-down bus wash. *John T. Etches*

An unusual view from a building on the north side of Bournemouth Square, showing the size of the bus station and the new office accommodation added during 1959. *John T. Etches*

7. THE 1960s

As the 1960s dawned, political preferences were once again beginning to have an effect on the bus industry. By now the Conservative Party had been in power for nearly a decade and was becoming increasingly concerned at the problems being experienced at the British Transport Commission. Back in 1950 British Railways was only just able to provide a surplus of revenue before meeting interest and other charges, and by 1962 performance would fall to an all-time low, resulting in the BTC's total loss of a staggering £143.6 million (approximately £1,900 million at 2006 values). A 1960 White Paper entitled 'Reorganisation of the Nationalised Transport Undertakings' claimed that the activities of the BTC were so large and diverse that it was virtually impossible to run them effectively. The BTC

was abolished under the 1962 Transport Act, which also saw the establishment of five new public authorities, the Transport Holding Co (THC) being responsible for bus-operating companies. Hants & Dorset was thus now a THC subsidiary but, as in 1947, the passenger noticed little change.

Although financial links with the railways had now been severed, British Railways officials still held directorships of Hants & Dorset — and would continue to do so for some years. Early in 1964 David Deacon, General Manager of neighbouring Wilts & Dorset, resigned and joined the Tilling Board. On 1 April his opposite number at Hants & Dorset, Douglas Morrison, became responsible for both the red buses of Wilts & Dorset and the green of Hants & Dorset. In 1965 the registered office of

▲ A busy scene at Bournemouth bus station, with two Bristol-engined double-deckers competing for centre stage. Lodekka 1343 (LRU 73) has just arrived from Ringwood on the 12 as KSW 1294 (KRU 960) readies itself for the 45min journey to Wimborne. *Terry Williams*

The desire to reduce staffing costs meant that the half-cab single-deckers, which required a driver and conductor, were soon seen as obsolete, and a rebuilding programme was instigated. The 1952 LL6Bs were rebuilt as forward-entrance, full-front buses, with cut-down bulkhead to allow one-man operation. No 787 (KRU 993) is seen in Southampton on 18 January 1964, five years after conversion. *M. A. Penn*

Seen in Southampton on the same day is sister vehicle 785 (KRU 991). Initially fitted with a similar front, it gained this modified design, similar to that fitted by ECW to Bristol SC coaches, in 1963. *M. A. Penn*

Wilts & Dorset was combined with that of Hants & Dorset at The Square, Bournemouth, although the two companies were managed as separate units.

In 1966 the THC acquired Shamrock & Rambler, the long-established Bournemouth coach operator, and its Charlie's Cars subsidiary. Formed following the merger of Shamrock Coaches and Bournemouth Rambler in April 1924, Shamrock & Rambler had in 1929 become a subsidiary of Keith & Boyle (London), adopting the orange-and-cream livery of sister operator Orange Luxury. In 1952 control of Keith & Boyle's coaching interests passed to the George Ewer and United Service Transport group, and it was the sale of UST shares to the Tilling Association which effectively nationalised Shamrock & Rambler. Shamrock & Rambler had taken over Charlie's Cars in 1963 and by 1966 had garages in Bournemouth, Southampton and the Isle of Wight.

During 1967 and 1968 the THC acquired four Isle of Wight-based coach operators — Crinage, Randall, Holmes Saloon and Fountain — which were all placed under Shamrock & Rambler control. Following the formation of the National Bus Company the Isle of Wight operations would pass to Southern Vectis, retaining the Fountain Coaches name and orange livery.

On the vehicular front, attention turned early in the 1960s to converting the ECW-bodied Bristol L coaches for bus use. As these were already full-fronted, conversion was a little more straightforward than had been the case with the Portsmouth Aviation versions: the workshops simply powered the front sliding door, cut the bulkhead down to allow fare collection and added destination-blind equipment. Some retained their coach seating.

In considering the vehicles being purchased new in the 1960s we need to go back to 1958, to witness the arrival of the first Bristol MW,

In 1960 attention turned to the Portsmouth Aviation-bodied coaches, a number of which were sent to ECW for complete rebodying. The first four to go were from the rear-entrance batch delivered in 1949, which returned lengthened to 30ft and fitted with 39 seats but retained their AEC engines. No 664 (JRU 67) is seen at Southampton in June 1968. *Bob Gray*

Similar treatment befell 14 of the forward-entrance Portsmouth Aviation coaches, which in addition to being lengthened and rebodied had their original Gardner engines exchanged with Bristol units from Lodekkas. A rear view of 672 (KEL 67) at Southampton in September 1969 shows the result of the transformation. *Bob Gray*

During their long lives the ECW-bodied Bristol L coaches of 1951 underwent various modifications. In 1958 sliding window vents replaced the wind-down originals, and six years later all were converted for bus use, which included the fitting of destination equipment and second-hand bus seats. Seen at Fareham in October 1967, 697 (KRU 998), one of the LWL6B versions, makes a handsome rural single-decker.
Bob Gray

The effect of a recent shower followed by a burst of bright sunshine creates a lovely image of Bristol MW6G coach 902 (FEL 426D) resting in Bournemouth bus station on 12 September 1970.
Phil Davies

The first MWs were delivered in 1959 and comprised three buses and half a dozen coaches. With antimacassars embroidered with an H&D monogram, coach-bodied 869 (YEL 228) poses for the ECW photographer to demonstrate the attractive products emerging from Lowestoft during this period.
S. J. Butler collection

successor to the LS. By now Hants & Dorset was buying very few new single-deck buses, preferring to buy coaches that could be adapted to bus use later in life, and by 1962 all new coaches were being specified with bus-type power doors to make the eventual conversion a little easier. Exactly 60 MWs were bought new, of which only 14 were to bus specification.

In 1964 the MWs had been joined by their new big rear-engined brother, the RE. Two 36ft-long monsters with ECW's coach bodywork entered the fleet that year on extended tours and were the only rear-engined vehicles until four more REs, but with Duple bodies, arrived in 1967. For now the first pair were to remain the only 36ft vehicles, as the latest deliveries were of the shorter and extremely unusual 33ft RESH6G type, of which only 11 were built (nine of them bodied by Duple). Seven more Duple-bodied RE coaches arrived in 1968 and 1969, though these were 36ft RELH6Gs.

Hants & Dorset's only single-deckers with the horizontal Bristol AHW engine were four LS6B coaches acquired from Southern Vectis in 1968. Seen at Southampton Central station in April 1968 on the shuttle service to the Royal Pier for the Isle of Wight steamer service is 845 (JDL 758), which had been converted for bus use before entering service. *B. C. Coward*

What can one say about this beautiful piece of British engineering? The original Bristol RE coach was a truly handsome vehicle, and the pair purchased by Hants & Dorset in 1964 looked especially fine in the company's dignified coach livery. Not only were they the first rear-engined vehicles but they were also the first built to the recently permitted 36ft length. Sadly both were to perish in the Bournemouth fire, but 898 (AEL 6B) is seen in happier times, on a staff outing to London in June 1969. *Bob Gray*

On the double-deck front nothing but Lodekkas entered the fleet. In 1960 the original LD type was superseded by the flat-floor FS, which did away with the LD's slightly sunken lower-deck gangway. There was a little variety when a batch of six uncommon 30ft-long, 70-seat rear-entrance FLs entered service at the beginning of 1962, soon followed by another seven. Rumour has it that these were originally intended to be forward-entrance FLFs, the first examples of which did not enter service with Hants & Dorset until 1965. All Lodekkas delivered from the end of 1961 had the Cave-Brown-Cave heating system, and a number featured illuminated offside advertisements. A mixture of Bristol and Gardner engines was specified, although the last 11 FLFs, delivered in 1967, were unusually fitted with Leyland O.600 engines and semi-automatic transmission.

By the end of 1964, following withdrawal of the last Leyland Titan, the fleet was made up entirely of Bristols, 483 being allocated to nine garages.

The FS Lodekka replaced the original LD type and featured a flat lower saloon floor and rear air suspension. It could be identified by the straight (rather than curved) lower edge to the cab windows and by the longer window bays. The differences are apparent when 1464 (4387 LJ) is compared with the LD waiting behind at Bournemouth.
Gary Baker

A damp Southampton bus station is the setting for one of the rare FL-type Lodekkas. A batch of six Bristol-engined FL6Bs arrived in 1961, a second intake, with Gardner power units, arriving the following year. The crew of FL6G 1483 (7683 LJ) have a quick chat before setting off on the 50min run to Fawley.
Alan O. Watkins

▲ In 1965 the company took delivery of its first forward-entrance Lodekka, which type was to be the standard choice of double-decker for the next three years. With the driver just about to shut his door ready for a run on the 48 to Southampton, six-month-old 1539 (FLJ 156D), new in February 1966, is seen in Winchester bus station. *D. A. P. Janes*

▶ From 1967 the registration suffix letter changed on 1 August. Four days after the change brand-new 1556 (KRU 223F) stands at Poole bus station, in a scene much changed since the building of the Poole Arts Centre across the road. *Phil Davies*

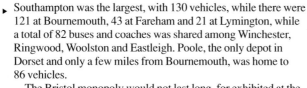

Although these ECW-bodied Bristol double-deckers — seen at Bournemouth *c*1966 — appear quite standardised, K type 1252 (JEL 271) has a Gardner engine, similar 1229 (JEL 248) has AEC power, and FS-type Lodekka 1478 (7678 LJ) is fitted with a Bristol unit. The differently coloured fleet-number plates reveal that the Ks are based at Bournemouth and that 1478 (with black numerals on a blue base) is a Poole bus.
D. A. P. Janes

From the summer of 1962 the cream band immediately below the upper-deck windows started to disappear. Displaying the simplified livery at Southampton in September 1967 is Bristol K6B 1259 (KEL 702).
Bob Gray

Southampton was the largest, with 130 vehicles, while there were 121 at Bournemouth, 43 at Fareham and 21 at Lymington, while a total of 82 buses and coaches was shared among Winchester, Ringwood, Woolston and Eastleigh. Poole, the only depot in Dorset and only a few miles from Bournemouth, was home to 86 vehicles.

The Bristol monopoly would not last long, for exhibited at the 1966 Commercial Motor Show was a Strachans Pacemaker-bodied Bedford VAM destined to become Hants & Dorset 824 (HRU 695E). With only 33 seats but with standing room for 25, this bus managed to offer a total capacity only two less than the number of seats available in a Bristol FS double-decker, but without a conductor. A further three were delivered in 1967, along with a fifth similar bus but bodied by Willowbrook, and 10 more Willowbrook-bodied VAMs, dual-door 40-seaters, arrived in 1968, similar vehicles joining Wilts & Dorset. The choice of chassis may have come as a surprise, but Bedford coaches had for many years been a feature of Shamrock & Rambler, and, at the time, Wilts & Dorset and a number of other larger operators

No 825 (JLJ 51E), one of the five Strachans-bodied Bedford VAMs, prepares to leave Bournemouth for Canford Cliffs, one of the more upmarket areas of Poole, in 1969.
D. A. P. Janes

Along with the Strachans-bodied Bedfords came 10 with Willowbrook bodies. August 1974 finds 1512 (MRU 70F) waiting in the rain at Bournemouth. Renumbered from 3007 in 1971, this neat little bus has a modified front for use on the Sandbanks ferry and now has just five months to go before being sold. *Bill Potter*

were experimenting with lighter-weight, lower-cost products from Bedford in particular. However, it is probably fair to say that only the most ardent Bedford fan would appreciate a long ride in one of these vehicles. Their noisy front engines, rattling away alongside the driver, made the entrance awkward, and the lightweight construction, while making the fuel costs look less scary, meant a choppy ride when lightly loaded. Further Bedfords arrived right at the end of the decade, this time for the coach fleet, Duple supplying its Viceroy body on three VALs which looked rather smart in Tilling green and cream.

Normality soon returned with the arrival of the first Bristol RE and LH buses. A very civilised vehicle, the RE was purchased in both bus and dual-purpose coach-seated form. The latter were single-door and finished in bus livery with the addition of a cream roof, making a most attractive vehicle; one example was also painted into normal dual-purpose livery of cream above the waistband and green below. The RE buses were dual-door, as were initial deliveries of the LH, but it was soon realised that the extra door was unnecessary on such a small vehicle, and from 1970 only the bus-seated REs would be delivered with two doors.

In 1968 came a return to Bristol-built saloons, with the arrival of the first RE buses. Five were built to single-door layout and fitted with coach seats for longer services, but 841 (NLJ 871G) is seen on local route 14 to the quaintly named Lilliput. *Bob Gray*

Alongside the dual-purpose REs came bus-seated examples with dual doors. About to embark on the lengthy run from Bournemouth to Weymouth in April 1969 is 835 (NLJ 824G). *Bob Gray*

The author has no reason for including this rear-end shot of brand-new Bristol RELL/ECW 3013 (PLJ 744G) at Fareham other than that he particularly likes it, the apparent reluctance of photographers to record this aspect making such views all the more special. *Bob Gray*

For a while the dual-door layout became an obsession, the Bedfords, RE buses and even the first LHs being built to this layout. The first LH was 828 (NLJ 817G), seen in June 1969 at Southampton. *Bob Gray*

Later deliveries of Bristol RE coaches had Duple coachwork. New in the summer of 1968, RELH 916 (MRU 124F) is seen in Bath on Saturday 13 February 1971. *Phil Davies*

The final RELH coaches had an updated Duple Commander body with a neater and altered side trim. Seen at Bournemouth bus station in 1972, No 1058 (REL 742H) was the last delivered before a switch was made to the Leyland Leopard. The RE coaches were an unlucky type; two were destroyed by fire in separate incidents during 1970, and a further four, including 1058, were burnt out in the Bournemouth fire.
D. A. P. Janes

8. NBC

In 1968 yet another Transport Act spelled change for the bus industry — and this time passengers *would* notice the difference. Harold Wilson's first Labour Government had come to power in 1964 and envisaged integrating public passenger transport across the UK. London Transport was placed under the direct control of the Greater London Council, and regional Passenger Transport Executives were to be set up. A new Scottish Transport Group was to look after the Scottish Bus Group and ferry operations, plus MacBrayne's haulage interests, while in England and Wales the National Bus Company (NBC) had the task of taking over the former THC operations.

Anticipating the new legislation, BET, having held out so strongly against nationalisation, finally decided it no longer wished to be involved with UK buses and late in 1967 sold its bus

interests to THC for £35 million. This paved the way for NBC to take over and integrate the THC and BET operations. Hants & Dorset became an NBC subsidiary on 1 January 1969.

In May 1969 Shamrock & Rambler's Southampton-based tours fleet of eight coaches (three AEC Reliances, three Bedford SB5s and two Bedford VAL14s, all with Duple bodies) was merged with Hants & Dorset's, which also transferred four of its own, painted into Shamrock & Rambler livery, to augment it. There were plans to expand this process but, in keeping with the foot-shuffling which began to afflict the industry, all would be back under the control of Shamrock & Rambler by August 1973.

From 1 June 1969 the legal lettering on Wilts & Dorset buses was changed to 'Hants & Dorset Motor Services', and all future deliveries would arrive bearing Bournemouth-issued

▲ The first second-hand vehicles purchased for over 20 years were a quartet of Bristol LS6B coaches acquired from Southern Vectis in 1968. Seen trundling across the Hampshire countryside in June 1970 is 844 (JDL 757), by now fitted with bus seats and a five-cylinder Gardner engine. *Phil Davies*

registrations, EL, LJ and RU replacing the traditional AM, HR, MW and WV Wiltshire marks. Effectively, the vehicles now operating from Amesbury, Andover, Basingstoke, Blandford, Pewsey and Salisbury depots were Hants & Dorset buses in Tilling red with Wilts & Dorset fleetnames.

A side-effect of the Transport Act was increased staffing problems for a number of companies, of which Hants & Dorset was one. A reduction in the permitted hours drivers could work meant that covering duties with staff on overtime or rest-day working was no longer possible. This created an immediate staff shortage and, not surprisingly, was not welcomed by the road staff, who found their earning potential dropping. As a result costs increased, many services had to be cancelled, and reliability suffered. In 1970 Hants & Dorset recorded its first ever deficit.

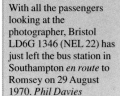

With all the passengers looking at the photographer, Bristol LD6G 1346 (NEL 22) has just left the bus station in Southampton *en route* to Romsey on 29 August 1970. *Phil Davies*

One of six 30ft-long Lodekkas delivered to Tilling Group companies in late 1957, Gardner-engined LDL6G 1406 (UEL 727) arrives at Southampton on 27 June 1970. The sun visor fitted above the driver's cab window was an H&D peculiarity that usually appeared on vehicles after their first repaint. *Phil Davies*

The Plaxton Panorama Elite was one of the finest coach bodies ever produced, and Hants & Dorset's first example looked especially handsome in Tilling green and cream. Leyland Leopard 934 (SRU 999H) is seen loaded with enthusiastic holidaymakers at Bournemouth in July 1970. *Phil Davies*

NBC's first birthday was celebrated by the purchase of the Gosport & Fareham Omnibus Co, which was put under the wing of Hants & Dorset. However, as the borough of Gosport had the right to provide bus services of its own, Gosport & Fareham's services were protected by statute, and the fleet retained its 'Provincial' identity and continued to operate the services in its own area. The private-hire and contract work was transferred to Hants & Dorset, and although Provincial had its head office moved to Bournemouth and was now administered by Hants & Dorset, day-to-day control was still exercised from Hoeford, the fleet continuing to operate as a separate entity.

Despite Hants & Dorset's worsening financial position there was some good news. Major redevelopment of Poole town centre had included the construction of a new shopping centre and bus station, and in 1970 the Poole allocation moved to a brand-new depot at the rear of the new complex. Another significant development of 1970 was the arrival of Hants & Dorset's first Leyland Leopard coach, delivered in June. This fine-looking vehicle was also the first Leyland purchased by Hants & Dorset since 1949 and the company's first-ever Plaxton-bodied vehicle.

Coaching aside, vehicle policy remained much the same as under the previous regime, but the arrival of half-a-dozen Roe-bodied Daimler Fleetlines in June 1971 came as a bit of a surprise. These had originally been ordered by Gosport & Fareham, but a need to replace the last highbridge Bristol Ks on the Bournemouth–Poole services meant that a swap was made with a similar number of REs on order for Hants & Dorset. The Fleetlines, Hants & Dorset's first rear-engined double-deckers,

The longest day of 1970, 21 June, finds brand-new Bristol RELL 3036 (SRU 830H) leaving Salisbury, bound for Bournemouth. *Phil Davies*

The simple addition of a cream roof to the standard livery gave the dual-purpose REs an elegant look. Showing off its fine lines in Bournemouth in May 1971 is recently delivered 3048 (UEL 564J), pulling up Exeter Road with The Square in the background. *Phil Davies*

Brand-new Bristol LH6L 3053 (TRU 222J) stands at East Boldre, near Brockenhurst, on 12 September 1970. The 112 from Lymington to Hythe provided a connection with the ferry across Southampton Water to the city's Royal Pier.
Phil Davies

were impressive-looking buses in full Tilling green with traditional fleetnames and were numbered 1901-6 — the first signal that a further fleet renumbering was about to take place.

In essence a huge tidying-up exercise, the new scheme involved allocating blocks of numbers to different types of vehicle. Coaches were numbered from 1001 upwards, front-engined double-decker buses from 1101 (Bristol FS from 1101, FL and FLF from 1201, LD from 1401), lightweight single-deckers (Bedford VAM and Bristol LH) from 1501, larger single-deckers from 1601 (RE from 1603, MW from 1801) and the Fleetlines from 1901. The remaining Bristol KSWs, which were in the process of being replaced, were numbered ahead of the earliest Lodekkas, as 1338-99. Similarly, the LS single-deckers were slotted in before the MWs as 1762-99. It will be noted that 1601 and 1602 were not used. These were reserved for the original pair of RE coaches (now renumbered 1051/2), which

were intended to be converted to bus specification during the mid-1970s. However, tragic events later in the decade meant these numbers were destined to remain unused.

The Wilts & Dorset fleet was also renumbered using the same system but with fleet numbers 1000 lower than the H&D fleet. This was a clever way of keeping the fleet separate but retaining a link between the types.

The new numbers were applied in bright yellow transfers and replaced the coloured metal plates used since 1956. To show a vehicle's home depot, a series of coloured discs was employed. Vehicles operating in the Eastern Area had yellow discs. Southampton, the main Eastern Area depot, was identified by a single yellow disc, while other depots in the area used two discs — the yellow Area disc and a separate depot one. Winchester, for example, used yellow and orange. For the Western Area white was the dominant colour, Poole using the solitary disc. Wilts & Dorset

◄ The six Roe-bodied Daimler Fleetlines diverted from Provincial were attractive vehicles. With passengers eager to disembark, 1905 (VRU 128J), displaying both Tilling and NBC-style fleetnames, enters the bus station at Bournemouth. *D. A. P. Janes*

▼ How many times has that parking meter been knocked by buses manœuvring around Grosvenor Square depot? The Lodekka is dominant in this view, a number of LD and FS types being seen resting between duties. Of interest, in the centre of the yard, are 1438 (YRU 77) and 1452 (5679 EL), from the first batch of FSs identifiable by the lack of Cave-Brown-Cave grilles. *D. A. P. Janes*

Bournemouth bus station in 1972, with a variety of Bristol KSW, RE, MW and LD types along with a couple of Bedfords to add some variety. *Ian Allan Library*

was now regarded as the company's Northern Area and used blue discs, Salisbury being the principal depot. However, Blandford, previously a Wilts & Dorset depot, used white and grey discs, having been transferred to Hants & Dorset's Western Area; this made sense, as it is nearer to Poole than to Salisbury.

As we shall see, while the 1970s are seldom regarded as the glory days of any bus company, the variety of vehicles to enter the enlarged Hants & Dorset fleet certainly made the decade one of the more interesting from the bus enthusiast's point of view. The first surprise turned up right at the end of 1971, when a pair

of Willowbrook-bodied Leyland Panthers arrived from Maidstone & District. Over the next few months 33 of these rear-engined beasts were received, being shared between the Hants and Wilts fleets, at Basingstoke, Salisbury and Southampton. Very different from anything else operated, these were also the first buses acquired from a former BET subsidiary (now, of course, part of NBC), having been new to M&D during the period 1965-7. Preparing them for service took a while, the final examples not entering traffic until December 1972. Four of the H&D examples entered service in Maidstone & District green.

It is interesting to compare the difference in height between a highbridge KSW and a lowbridge version alongside a low-height Lodekka, which employed the same gangway layout as the highbridge bus. This scene was recorded at Southampton shortly after the 1971 fleet renumbering and the replacement of the fleet-number plates by transfers and coloured allocation discs. *D. A. P. Janes*

The 1971 renumbering scheme took effect on 5 September, the new numbers being applied to buses a few days beforehand, in readiness. Seen in its home town on 4 September is Ringwood-based LD6G 1419 (YRU 58), with pink fleet-number plate showing its original number beneath its new identity (1482) with white and pink discs. The next morning the screwdriver would come out . . . *Phil Davies*

Saturday 4 September 1971 was the last day of service 124 from Ringwood to Hurn, a tiny village near Bournemouth that boasts three houses, a shop and an airport. Seen at Matchams on the final journey is Bristol MW5G 812 (2714 EL), which would be renumbered 1811 the following day. *Phil Davies*

Although the first ex-Maidstone & District Leyland Panther entered service in March 1972 the last did not do so until the end of the year. This meant that these vehicles included the last to enter service in Tilling green and the first to carry NBC red. One of the green examples was 1685 (DKE 265C), seen at Grosvenor Square, Southampton. *D. A. P. Janes*

In contrast 16 of the Panthers donned Tilling red and joined Wilts & Dorset. Seen at Salisbury in August 1974 is 699 (JKK 210E), with cream Hants & Dorset fleetnames. *Bill Potter*

9. RED IS THE COLOUR

The year 1972 was a big one for the National Bus Company. It appeared that the sorting out of the former Tilling and BET fleets was complete, and a number of decisions were made. The most obvious was the introduction of a corporate image, to be used throughout the organisation. Buses were to be painted either leaf green or poppy red, while coaches, whether on express or tour work, would be all-over white with large ''NATIONAL' fleetnames. Vehicles considered capable of either bus or coach work would be in a dual-purpose livery of either red or green with a white upper half.

There was also a number of reorganisations in the set-up of individual companies. In the same year that Thames Valley and Aldershot & District were merged to form Alder Valley, Wilts & Dorset and Hants & Dorset were fully amalgamated as ...

Hants & Dorset. The combined fleet was also to adopt a standard NBC livery — poppy red, rather than the leaf green which most people would have expected. *Now* the passengers boarding their buses deep in the New Forest would notice a difference. The choice of red rather than green was in deference to Wilts & Dorset — since 1969 merely a trading name but which now saw its identity disappear completely — but still came as a surprise. Provincial, ever on its own, adopted leaf green.

Fairly soon NBC-style fleetnames were applied to all vehicles, generally being in cream on those buses still retaining Tilling-style liveries. The first vehicles delivered after the change to poppy red were the final batch of REs ordered for the Wilts & Dorset fleet, which entered service in Tilling red but with white waistbands and NBC-style Hants & Dorset fleetnames.

Seen at Bournemouth in August 1973, Bristol LS5G bus 1784 (SRU 974) has but a short time to go until retirement. Although the vehicle retains the traditional fleetname, the NBC image is slowly starting to appear with the advertisement above the side windows, grey wheels and a poppy-red Lodekka sneaking into view.
D. A. P. Janes

The traditional underlined fleetname began to be replaced in 1972 by NBC-style block lettering. On single-deckers this was usually applied to the roof coving, but due to the styling of former coach 1834 (2688 RU) the side panels had to be used. Seen at Bournemouth in August 1973, this vehicle would not be withdrawn until November 1976, by which time it was the last in Tilling green. *D. A. P. Janes*

Now relegated to school work, ex-Wilts & Dorset Bristol MW 832 (134 AMW), seen in Salisbury in August 1974, carries cream NBC-style names on its Tilling-red-and-cream livery. The 1971 renumbering made merging the two fleets relatively simple, all the vehicles retaining their allocated numbers. *Bill Potter*

By the end of 1972 the first new vehicles to carry poppy red had been delivered. These were the company's first Bristol VRTs and arrived carrying their booked fleet numbers, 1301-6. However, these were soon changed to 3301-6. Similarly, the first Leyland Nationals, originally intended to be 701-4 in the Wilts & Dorset fleet, entered service in the early part of 1973 as 3601-4. A further example of the policy change was evident in the 1973 batch of Bristol LHs. These entered service as 3501-10 with registration numbers DEL 537-46L, the last Wilts & Dorset LH having been numbered 536. These changes demonstrated that both fleets were now completely merged.

Repainting of existing vehicles soon got underway, and by the end of 1973 examples of Lodekkas, LSs, MWs and REs from both fleets were in poppy red. The first white coach had emerged from the paintshops in January.

In 1973 a great deal of variety was added to the fleet. On 29 April the services and vehicles of King Alfred Motor Services of Winchester, one of the oldest-established independents in Southern England, were acquired, bringing an assortment of 37 buses, coaches and minibuses, almost all of which were new types for Hants & Dorset. They included AEC Renowns and Bridgemasters, Leyland Atlanteans and Tiger Cubs as well as more Panthers and, the newest vehicles in the fleet, three Metro-Scanias. The seven minibuses were 12-seat Ford Transits.

At the end of the year the first of a series of vehicle hires was indicated by the arrival of 10 Southern Vectis LD6G-type Lodekkas; these were allocated fleet numbers 3488-97 for their stay, which in some cases lasted more than a year. Shorter visits were made by Southampton Corporation AEC Swifts (used in Bournemouth) and Bournemouth Daimler Roadliners and Leyland Titans (in Southampton and Poole). In addition, Western National supplied Bristol MW coaches

A little confused, MW 819 carries both Hants & Dorset and Wilts & Dorset fleetnames at Salisbury, also in August 1974. *Bill Potter*

A number of the ancillary vehicles and training buses carried joint fleetnames. Demonstrating this at Salisbury in August 1974 is ex-Wilts & Dorset Bristol KSW 335 (HHR 62), now numbered 9091 for its training duties. *Bill Potter*

Colourful Bournemouth. August 1974 finds Bristol FLF 1250 (HRU 678E), recently repainted in poppy red, sharing the bus station with a green LD and orange ex-Wilts & Dorset FLF 220 (JMR 815F) in an overall advertisement scheme for the Coal Board. *Bill Potter*

Wilts & Dorset had a penchant for Bedfords, both as buses and coaches, and a number survived the 1972 merger. Outshopped in National white during May 1974, Duple-bodied YRQ 21 (VLJ 413J) is seen at Salisbury in 1976.
James Prince collection

From 1970 the Leyland Leopard became the standard choice for the coach fleet, a number being acquired new and second-hand. No 934 (SRU 999H), seen here after being repainted in National white and renumbered 1059, was the first Leyland delivered since 1949.
James Prince collection

Stranger in the camp! Just after the takeover, Bristol KSW6B 1361 (KRU 964) shares the King Alfred yard at Winchester Chesil station with 159 JHX, an AEC Regent V ex-demonstrator which was not included in the sale. *D. A. P. Janes*

Of the vehicles taken over from King Alfred virtually none was standard within the Hants & Dorset fleet, although a number gained poppy red and stayed for a while. Seen in Winchester, No 2211 (595 LCG) was one of two AEC Renowns which lasted until 1976. *Bill Potter*

The ex-King Alfred routes were renumbered into the 180s, and the vehicles acquired mostly fitted with three-track number displays to accommodate the new scheme. Showing these changes in Winchester is 2652 (413 FOR), a Willowbrook-bodied Leyland Leopard dating from 1962. *Bill Potter*

Unusual purchases were five ex-Maidstone & District Atlanteans which joined the fleet in 1973. No 3996 (532 HKJ) makes an imposing sight returning to Basingstoke from Bramley. *Bill Potter*

▲ bearing Royal Blue fleetnames, AEC Regents still in traditional Devon General livery and a pair of Tilling-green Lodekkas.

To boost the bus fleet 16 Lodekkas, a solitary Bristol MW coach (from Lincolnshire) and six Leyland Atlanteans (from Maidstone & District) were acquired in 1973/4. One of the Atlanteans was used for spares, but the others provided useful extra capacity on one-man-operated routes, initially around Basingstoke. The Lodekkas included the company's first LD5Gs (from Eastern National) and a mix of forward- and rear-entrance FS types from Southdown, the forward-entrance FSFs being

another first. The Atlanteans would not last long, joining Western National in 1976 in exchange for a quartet of elderly coaches — two Bristol REs (used for spares) and a pair of ex-Southdown Leyland Leopards. Further second-hand coaches were more Leopards, but with a variety of bodywork. Duple-bodied examples came from North Western, unusual Weymann Castilians from Southdown and, in 1975, Alexander Y types (new to North Western) from National Travel (North West). Later in the decade further Duple-bodied Leopards would come from Southdown and some Plaxton examples from Ribble.

Two months after the takeover a pair of Eastern National Bristol Lodekkas were acquired to help out on King Alfred services. Equipped with a King Alfred blind, 3498 (XVX 29) is seen in green with a white band, which livery it would retain until withdrawal in February 1975. *D. A. P. Janes*

Acquired from North Western in 1973 and entering service in an unusual livery of white and poppy red is 3003 (FJA 227D), a 1966 Duple-bodied Leyland Leopard. After leaving the fleet at the end of 1976 it would be purchased by Cooper of Stockton Heath, fitted with a new Plaxton body and re-registered BJP 642T. *James Prince collection*

The purchase of a number of elderly Lodekkas during the mid-1970s added a number of new variants to the fleet. The forward-entrance FSF was a rare type, but six ex-Southdown examples entered service during 1975. Seen in Marlborough is Pewsey-allocated 3477 (VAP 33). *Bill Potter*

Other acquisitions, albeit under different circumstances, included three dual-door Leyland Nationals from London Country, received in September 1973 in exchange for the King Alfred Metro-Scanias (which would fit in with similar buses already in service in Stevenage), and six Bristol saloons — five LSs and an RE — from Western National, upon takeover of the latter's Swanage-area services in January 1974. Interestingly, the RE was Hants & Dorset's only single-door version with bus seats, while the Nationals were to be its only dual-door examples.

On the debit side, in one of the many upheavals that were to take place during the NBC era the Shamrock & Rambler vehicles and the Holdenhurst Road coach station had in 1973 passed from Hants & Dorset control to National Travel (South West). Local-government reorganisation in 1974 had little direct impact but meant that Hants & Dorset's head office now found itself in Dorset, to which county Bournemouth and Christchurch had been transferred.

Vehicle shortages in the bus industry were rife throughout the 1970s, and the arrival of these extra vehicles helped alleviate some of the problems. They also helped see off a number of the more senior members of the fleet, which in 1974 meant the withdrawal of the last Bristol KSWs and LSs. Among the final few KSWs that hung on into 1974 were former Wilts & Dorset 380 (JHR 959) and 381 (JMW 243), the last lowbridge-bodied Bristols still in service with NBC. Seventeen-year-old 1794 (UEL 737) was the final LS to be withdrawn, in December 1974, two months before the last Bedford bus, 1509 (MRU 67F).

Two of the 14 surviving Wilts & Dorset KSWs are seen in this January 1973 view at Basingstoke, KSW5Gs 370/1 (HMW 447/8) both showing scars from the foliage around the Hampshire countryside. Both would be withdrawn later in the year, by which time they were among the last lowbridge buses with an NBC fleet.
P. R. Nuttall

The ECW-bodied Fords, with noisy front engines, manual gearboxes and awkward entrances, made Salisbury their home and were often to be seen at the bus station, loading up for a run across the Wiltshire countryside. Nos 3584/93 (RRU 584/93N) demonstrate.
James Prince collection

To supplement the ECW-bodied Fords, five Plaxton-bodied examples turned up in 1976. All were based at Salisbury and used on what became the Wiltsway network. No 3814 (NJT 831P) is seen returning to its home city in 1980. *James Prince collection*

Not the most popular vehicles, the three little Ford-based Alexander S-type minibuses were useful for local services such as the 110, which spent the day pottering around Lymington. No 2001 (PFX 237R) takes a break in the town's bus station. *James Prince collection*

It must be said that the plan had always been for the lightweight Bedfords to have a relatively short life in the fleet, and further lightweight vehicles arrived to replace them. It was now the turn of Bedford's great rival, Ford, to make an appearance. A batch of ECW-bodied front-engined R1014s joined the usual deliveries of Bristol VRs, LHs and Leyland Nationals and, looking like longer LHs, made Salisbury their home. The allocation was bolstered early in 1976 by the receipt of five Plaxton-bodied Ford R1014 buses, while an early attempt at the 27-seat midibus appeared in the shape of three Alexander (Belfast) S-type integrals based on Ford A-series running units. This is not a model Ford tends to remind people about and these potentially handy little buses led very short lives.

Open-top operation returned during the glorious summer of 1976 with the arrival from Southdown of four convertible-open-top Lodekkas for use around Bournemouth. These ran for two summers and retained their leaf-green livery. By November 1976 the entire fleet was in NBC livery, Hants & Dorset becoming the first operator in the South to achieve this. A minor variation appeared in 1976 whereby the double-N NBC symbol appeared in blue and red on a white square alongside the fleetname, in place of the plain white used previously. This first appeared on repainted buses in January, but new vehicles continued to arrive with the old white symbol for a few more months.

The company had already suffered some losses through fire back in 1974, when, in two separate incidents at Basingstoke depot, a number of vehicles, (including two of the ex-Maidstone & District Panthers and a pair of almost-new Leyland Nationals) were burnt out. But during the night of Saturday/Sunday 24/25 July 1976 disaster struck. Deep in the bowels of Bournemouth bus station a fire, believed to have started in a tyre store, engulfed the low-level coach station and destroyed a number of Western National and Hants & Dorset vehicles. The fire ultimately destroyed the bus station itself, as the structural damage was deemed uneconomic to repair. Eight Western National coaches were either burnt out or seriously damaged, while Hants & Dorset lost 10 vehicles. Eight of these were coaches — a Bristol MW, four REs and three Plaxton-bodied Leopards — the other casualties being one of the ex-King Alfred Ford Transit minibuses and an Austin Princess staff car. Regrettably the coach toll included both ECW-bodied RELHs and one of the rare Duple-bodied RESHs, all of which had been parked for the night shortly before the fire started.

Fortunately the buses parked on the higher level were driven to safety, mainly by a Bournemouth Transport driver making his way home after an evening out. But things were never the same again. The coach departures moved to the Shamrock & Rambler garage in Holdenhurst Road, which fulfilled this role until the opening of a new Travel Interchange at Bournemouth railway station in 1991. Buses were now using makeshift stops around The Square, the nearby Triangle acting as a focal point for staff and most services.

For the first few months vehicles were parked and fuelled at Bournemouth Corporation's Mallard Road depot, but arrangements were made to reacquire the old Royal Mews garage which had been vacated in 1959. This served as the new Bournemouth depot until 1980, when the allocation was moved to Poole. Gradually some services returned to the upper level of the bus station, but due to structural damage not all of the area could be used. The inevitable happened in 1980, when the last service left the bus station and the site was sold for redevelopment. Demolition followed soon afterwards, but incredibly, 30 years after the fire, wrangling continues over what should be done with the land.

◄ The morning after. Bournemouth bus station, Sunday 25 July 1976.
Lenston Gwynne

◄◄ After the Bournemouth fire buses were parked along various roads and into any odd corner that would accommodate them. Bristol VRT 3323 (JJT 435N), LH 3536 (ORU 536M), a dual-purpose RE and a Lodekka take refuge in the Town Hall car park. *Lenston Gwynne*

◄ Bournemouth Triangle became a makeshift bus station. Taking a rest between journeys are downgraded Bristol MW coach 1836 (2690 RU), dual-purpose RELL 1648 (XLJ 723K) and FS 1105 (5667 EL), while serving as a crew rest room is another downgraded MW coach, 1826 (1472 LJ). *Lenston Gwynne*

◄ Inspectors were kept busy letting passengers and staff know where to find their bus. Often to be found acting as crew transport were the ex-King Alfred Ford Transit minibuses; seen at the Triangle, 2047 (VOW 814J) awaits the call to help. *James Prince collection*

Such was the rush in arranging the new facilities at the Triangle that not everything was perfect ... 'accept' the buses, of course. *James Prince collection* ►

Built into the side of the bus station was a small arcade of shops, which remained open until the station closed completely in 1980. Would the ex-North Western Alexander-bodied Leyland Leopard be able to entice the lady pondering over the jewellery selection onto an afternoon excursion in this September 1976 view? *Ray Stenning*

Inside the reopened Norwich Avenue garage we find Bristol LH 1546 (XEL 832K) accompanying ex-Southdown convertible Lodekka 3485 (RPN 9). Presumably the single-deck restriction would be adhered to when 3485 had its roof fitted! *James Prince collection*

Saturday 29 November 1980 was an emotional day for both staff and
enthusiasts, this being the date crew operation ended. Bristol FL6G
1210 (7685 LJ) was chosen to perform the last rites and is seen,
suitably decorated, waiting at Bournemouth bus station. Later that
evening it would become the last vehicle to use the bus station.
James Prince collection

Framed by the magnificent exit to Winchester 'Omnibus Station' are Leyland National 3670 (NEL 123P), leaving for Andover, and Bristol FLF6L 1260 (KRU 237F), loading up on the 48 to Southampton — a regular haunt of these unusual Leyland-engined FLFs. *James Prince collection*

A glance inside Southampton's Winchester Road bodyworks during 1978 reveals a couple of Bristol FLFs undergoing remedial work to their rear ends, this being a common weak-spot on the type. *Patrick Miller*

10. MAPPING OUT THE FUTURE

Although Bournemouth would never be the same again, Hants & Dorset carried on with regular deliveries of Leyland Nationals, Bristol VRTs and LHs. The receipt of six new convertible VRTs to replace the ex-Southdown Lodekkas added a touch of interest. However, they would be used in open-top form only at the 1978 Epsom Derby, the open-top services having been taken over by Bournemouth Transport. Green buses returned to the area the following year, when six standard VRTs arrived from Southern Vectis and the convertibles went to the Isle of Wight in exchange.

In 1978 the National Bus Company came up with the Market Analysis Project (MAP), designed to carry out wide-ranging revisions to bus services following extensive market research and consultation with local-authority planners. The idea was to make each area self-sufficient, providing a reliable service to as many passengers as possible using as few vehicles as necessary. The concept was embraced wholeheartedly by Hants & Dorset.

MAP spread across the area in stages. Vehicles, bus stops and publicity were branded with the new identities, although the Hants & Dorset name remained dominant. The first to be unveiled was Venturebus, which hit the streets of Basingstoke in September 1979 and recalled the name of an old Basingstoke-area operator absorbed by Wilts & Dorset. It was followed a couple of months later by Andover-based Antonbus. January 1980 saw Salisbury-area services rebranded Wiltsway and what was virtually the former King Alfred area in Winchester become Wintonline. In Gosport and Fareham the Provincial name was used on both green and red buses from June 1980. The final two schemes were South Hants, in the Southampton/Eastleigh area, and South Wessex in Poole/Bournemouth, both launched before the end of 1980.

The exchange of Bristol VRTs with Southern Vectis was a protracted affair lasting from March until July 1979, and for a while the convertibles that were waiting to cross the water shared Poole bus station with green VRTs that had already made their home on the mainland. Convertible 3379 (the last to leave) and ex-Southern Vectis 3416 illustrate the point in July 1979. *James Prince collection*

The company's penultimate Leyland National, 3750 (FPR 66V), offers a ride to a New Forest pony in Burley. *James Prince collection*

Bearing Venturebus MAP names, Hants & Dorset's first Bristol VRT, Series 2 3301 (CRU 301L), enters Basingstoke bus station.
James Prince collection

Late in 1981 no fewer than 42 nearly new Bristol LHs were acquired from Bristol Omnibus and saw off almost all the native examples. Most, like 3827 (TTC 786T), seen in Bournemouth with South Wessex branding and fragmented fleetname, entered service in green.
James Prince collection

Three ex-London Country Leyland Nationals replaced the Metro-Scanias acquired from King Alfred. Still in Winchester on Wintonline work is 3626 (NPD 110L).
James Prince collection

Displaying South Hants MAP names at Southampton are Leyland National 3716 (VFX 982S) and Bristol LH 3564 (HJT 36N).
James Prince collection

Following the implementation of MAP schemes coach-seated Bristol VRT 3347 (NJT 33P), seen here in Salisbury, carried Antonbus names for Andover services.
James Prince collection

In 1980 a number of Provincial Bristol REs were transferred to the Hants & Dorset garage at Fareham and received Hants & Dorset fleetnames and numbers. Still green, 1661 (ECG 109K) shares Fareham bus station with a Southdown VRT.
James Prince collection

An agreement in 1978 between Hants & Dorset and Bournemouth Transport allowed 'Corporation' services into Poole for the first time since the trams left in 1935. Sneaking into Poole bus station during November 1980 is Leyland Fleetline 151, although the drivers seem more interested in the electronic destination display on Bristol VRT 3450 (KRU 850W) than the yellow intruder. *G. K. Gillberry*

If Bournemouth was not already bright enough with both yellow and red buses, the colourful overall advertising liveries which appeared on a number of vehicles added variety to the scene. Extolling the virtues of a car dealer, Bristol VRT 3455 (KRU 855W) is about to circumnavigate Bournemouth Square. *James Prince collection*

The MAP schemes were not a complete success. Comment was made on the way the surveys were carried out; most were done on the company's buses, and critics pointed out that it might have been more worthwhile to find out why people were *not* using the buses, rather than to ask those who were already doing so.

Meanwhile the coach fleet was not being ignored, each year receiving a regular delivery of new Plaxton-bodied Leyland Leopards. However, this was interrupted in 1978, when a pair of Duple-bodied Bedford YMTs arrived, and again in 1980, by

further lightweight Duple-bodied coaches — second-hand Ford R1114s from Southdown and PMT. Southdown supplied 12 more Duples in 1981, this time 11-year-old Commander IV-bodied Leopards.

In May 1981 an old friend was welcomed home. Yet another NBC reorganisation saw National Travel (South West) merged with Manchester-based National Travel (West) and most of the southern operations put under the charge of local subsidiaries. Shamrock & Rambler once again came under the control of

There was some variety to the coach fleet. In 1978 a pair of Duple Dominant II-bodied Bedfords arrived for use on local tours. Seen at Bournemouth on an excursion from Andover is 3066 (WPR 502S). *James Prince collection*

Five Duple Dominant-bodied Fords arrived from Southdown in 1980. Southampton-based 3005 (SCD 30N) is seen at Grosvenor Square in 1981. *James Prince collection*

Hants & Dorset. A collection of 39 coaches, mainly Leopards but also including a couple of AEC Reliances, with a mixture of Plaxton, Duple and Willowbrook bodywork, were renumbered into the Hants & Dorset series but retained Shamrock & Rambler fleetnames. Things had hardly settled down when three of the recently acquired Leopards were despatched to Plaxton for rebodying, emerging with new identities in time for the 1982 season.

Seven ECW-bodied Leopards delivered at the end of 1982 to boost the Shamrock & Rambler fleet proved to be historic vehicles. Not only did these include the last Leyland Leopard for NBC; they were also the last vehicles purchased new by Hants & Dorset. Events at Midland Red in 1981, when that company was split into smaller units, signalled a trend that NBC was to embrace; with more than 600 vehicles Hants & Dorset was an obvious target, and plans were unveiled to divide the company, with effect from 1 April 1983.

In 1981 three Leyland Leopards, two of which had been acquired from National Travel (South West), were sent to Plaxton for rebodying. The original Plaxton body of 3008 (SJA 409K), one of four Leopards acquired from National Travel (West) earlier in 1981, is seen awaiting disposal at Barton Park. *James Prince collection*

Transformation. Complete with Shamrock & Rambler names, the former 3008 proudly carries its new Plaxton body and new identity — 3052 (HBP 333X) — for National Holidays tours. It is seen waiting patiently at the rear of the ex-S&R coach station in Holdenhurst Road, Bournemouth, early in 1982. *James Prince collection*

The highest-numbered of 20 Leyland Fleetlines acquired from London Transport in 1982/3, 1926 (OJD 245R) entered service with Hampshire Bus after the division. Initially the new companies continued to use NBC standard liveries. *James Prince*

Perhaps the most unusual vehicle inherited by Shamrock & Rambler was 86 (TR 6147), a replica charabanc built by Hants & Dorset on the chassis of Bristol LH 3516 (NLJ 516M) and assuming the identity of 1929 Leyland Lion B86. It is seen during 1984, soon after repainting in S&R orange, outside Hants & Dorset's latter-day head office in Bournemouth. *James Prince*

The division resulted in three bus companies, a coach operator, an engineering company and a holding company finding their feet and attempting to stem the decline that had beset the great Hants & Dorset for so many years. It also reflected the new wave of thinking that had come with Margaret Thatcher's Conservative Government, elected in 1979, which frowned upon large state-owned companies. One of the early reforms had been to deregulate express coach services in 1980, and change was in the air for buses too. Although it was not necessarily realised at the time, new legislation would pave the way for deregulation of bus services in 1986 and for the privatisation of the National Bus Company. Each of the new subsidiaries was just the right size for potential purchasers to handle.

To operate services based in the former Wiltsway and South Wessex areas the Wilts & Dorset name was resurrected. This was the largest of the new companies and was privatised in June 1987 by a team formed by the local management. They went on to sell their thriving business to Go-Ahead Group in 2003.

Next in size was the unimaginatively titled Hampshire Bus. This was a combination of the former Antonbus, Venturebus, Wintonline and Hants MAP areas, with depots at Andover, Basingstoke, Winchester, Eastleigh and Southampton. It was privatised in April 1987, when it became the first former NBC operator to be purchased by the fledgling Stagecoach group.

The last vehicles to be delivered to Hants & Dorset were shared between Hampshire Bus and Wilts & Dorset. Ten former London Transport Leyland Fleetlines had been acquired in December 1982 for use at Poole, a further batch of 10 entering service at Southampton around the time of the split.

A revitalised Provincial took over the smallest of the three areas, corresponding to the Provincial MAP area. The company was privatised on 8 May 1987, when it was sold in a joint management/employees buy-out, and would pass to FirstGroup in October 1995.

Shamrock & Rambler took over the coach operation. Struggling from the start, the Southampton part of the company was reformed as Pilgrim Coaches in 1984, while the Basingstoke operations were absorbed by Hampshire Bus as Hampshire Coach. Pilgrim Coaches was privatised with Hampshire Bus but was closed down almost immediately by Stagecoach. By now operating solely from Bournemouth, Shamrock & Rambler was itself privatised in July 1987, when it was sold to Drawlane, part of the Salisbury-based Endless Holdings group. The previous year a minibus operation was started in Bournemouth under the Charlie's Cars name, but this ended in December 1988, and the loss of National Express contracts in April 1989 led to the closure of the business. Dorset Travel Services was set up to take over the National Express work, and later became a subsidiary of Bournemouth Transport.

Hants & Dorset Engineering Ltd, the servicing and maintenance arm, was based at Barton Park in Eastleigh but struggled to compete in the free market and ceased trading in January 1986. The only part to succeed was the stores operation, known as Hants & Dorset Distribution; this was sold in March 1987 and joined Frontsource Ltd, which would later become Bus Parts Ltd.

The last new vehicles received by Hants & Dorset were seven ECW-bodied Leyland Leopard coaches. Having passed via Shamrock & Rambler to the short-lived Pilgrim Coaches operation, one-time H&D 3094 (YEL 94Y) is seen on layover in Bournemouth, carrying an attractive version of NBC's 'Venetian blind' livery. *James Prince*

Initially Hants & Dorset Motor Services Ltd, based in Poole, remained as the holding company for the new operations and provided accounting and secretarial services. Once everything had been sold, its only function was to sort out the tax affairs that were left outstanding. Subsequently transferred to NBC's London headquarters, it went into voluntary liquidation in March 1988 and was finally wound up on 24 November 1990.

However, that is not quite the end. In May 1993 Wilts & Dorset purchased Blandford-based Damory Coaches. To do this it acquired a shelf company and renamed it Hants & Dorset Motor Services Ltd, trading as Damory Coaches. Given that the original Wilts & Dorset Motor Services was effectively snuffed out by its larger neighbour, there is a certain irony in the survival of 'Hants & Dorset' as a small, low-cost subsidiary of the new Wilts & Dorset Bus Company. Stretching the imagination slightly, one can still wait for a Hants & Dorset bus in deepest Dorset — although it will be very different from that first envisaged by Messrs Graham and French.

Looking exceptionally smart in Wilts & Dorset Bus Co's 'privatisation' livery is Bristol VR 3456 (KRU 856W), the last new double-decker delivered to Hants & Dorset. *James Prince*

A subsidiary of Wilts & Dorset, today's Hants & Dorset trades as Damory Coaches. Awaiting fuelling at Poole depot early in the evening of 21 March 2006 are a trio of Bristol VRs led by 5070 (GEL 686V), which had been new to the original Hants & Dorset some 26 years earlier. *James Prince*